This book will prove to be an invaluable resource to Christian parents seeking wisdom in navigating this transgender moment.

RYAN T. ANDERSON
Author of *When Harry Became Sally: Responding to the Transgender Moment*

Sharon James has written a book that is brief and powerful. In short scope, she reviews the current landscape of various issues around gender controversies, and gives the reader the information we need. She sets out to explain complicated issues in simple terms, and she succeeds. Helpful definitions, examples, and suggestions for further reading abound. Get this book and read it, and get lots of copies for friends and family to read as well. This little book reminds us that God created us male and female, and that that is very good.

MARK DEVER
Pastor, Capitol Hill Baptist Church, Washington, DC
President of 9Marks Ministries

God bless Sharon James for her willingness to tackle one of the most troubling social issues of our time. This book couldn't have come at a better time in our history. I encourage anyone who wants to get a better understanding to get your hands around this book. Find a quiet place, dig in and be changed by what you learn.

With easy-to-understand language and using a multidisciplinary approach, James shows how and why the gender-distressed may feel at odds with themselves and provides great insight and understanding to those among us who are burdened to help.

Indeed, as James so clearly articulates, we need to extend a great deal of compassion as we heed Christ's call to meet these people at their darkest depths and point the way to redemption and restoration.

WALT HEYER
Author and speaker (Sexchangeregret.com)

D0728400

In the beginning God made humanity male and female; today the devil seeks to destroy the good of humanity by deconstructing humanity into a hundred different 'genders'. This is a vital subject for the church to grasp. As someone who has been involved in the debate about gender identity and especially the issue of transgender, I have often been asked to write an accessible book on the subject for ordinary Christians. Now I don't need to. Sharon James' book more than fulfils that need. Though short, it is packed with all the information and background you will need to help you understand what is going on in our culture. Clearly written, well-informed, contemporary and biblical. Personally I would recommend that every Christian have a copy, and every church several. Superb!

DAVID ROBERTSON
Author and apologist (www.theweeflea.com)

This is a remarkable book, both for the range of material covered and its sharp insights into the dominant pathologies of our time. The reader will find herein helpful guides to the origins, history, terminology, and major theorists of the sexual revolution, specifically as it culminates in its latest iteration – that of the transgender movement. Sharon James presents vast amount of difficult material in an accessible, condensed form, helping the reader navigate the fog that surrounds gender theory and its political implications. But she offers more than just a description of how we arrived here: she also provides suggestions for further reading and a final chapter on how Christians should address the issue with both grace and truth. This is a book from which all parents, pastors, and the Christian public in general will greatly benefit.

CARL R. TRUEMAN
Professor, Grove City College, Grove City, Pennsylvania

No one in their right mind will enjoy reading this book. I found it chilling. But unless you are already well-versed in gender ideology then you need to read it, because this anti-God and ultimately anti-human ideology threatens to take over the western world (as a start), demanding not just tolerance but positive acceptance. If you think that maybe Christians are over-reacting or obsessed, then you should pay close attention to the roots of this movement described here, to its God-hating exaltation of the Self, and to the way in which it is coming to a school near you soon (if it isn't there already). Sharon James draws an important distinction between kindness toward those who struggle to accept the way God has made them and resistance to the ideology that would use them as pawns, but this accessible book is a direct and urgent call to stand firm against that ideology.

GARRY WILLIAMS
Director, Pastors' Academy, London Seminary, London

Compassion demands that we grasp the argument of this powerful yet uncomfortable book. Sharon James is persuasive as she shows us that 'Gender theory is a lie', and like all lies, it is causing damage, particularly to the vulnerable. This book will help congregations to have clarity where they might be feeling perplexed and it will also help us as we seek to minster in love to those who have been impacted. It will also equip us to reason with those who are promoting or accepting of the Gender Theory agenda. Sharon has done the church a great service.

GREG STRAIN
Senior Pastor, Spicer Street Church, St Albans, Hertfordshire
(Greg practiced as a Doctor before entering Christian ministry)

This comprehensive overview of gender ideology and the transgender movement – its roots, its demands, its contradictions and its increasingly pervasive influence on our society today – will help readers to better understand a central part of the culture wars we are facing. Sharon James explains simply some of the unprecedented threats to our freedom that come with gender ideology, and its roots in radical feminism, cultural marxism and the sexual revolution, which have all spread at astonishing speed. This contrasts starkly with God's good design of male and female. A challenging, confusing and complex topic is handled in an accessible, respectful and compassionate way, which will leave the reader with greater confidence in the truth that we have all been created male or female.

PHILIPPA TAYLOR
Head of Public Policy at Christian Medical Fellowship
Consultant on Bioethics

The clear message of this book is: 'The Emperor has no clothes!' Sharon James sets out the truth about transgender ideology, and calls Christians to awareness of the LGBTQ agenda. Gender theory is a dangerous lie and people are being hurt by it. *Gender Ideology* makes it clear that passivity and affirmation are not the way of love for individuals struggling with gender dysphoria. We must respond with respect that upholds God's good design for humanity. If you are a pastor, parent, teacher, student or friend, you should read this book.

KERI FOLMAR
Pastor's wife, the United Christian Church of Dubai
author of *The Good Portion: Scripture*

A powerful, eye-opening, gracious, and ultimately alarming book that will quickly give readers a deeper understanding of the deceptiveness of the modern 'gender identity' movement that is rapidly capturing our media, our laws, our schools, and our children – and even our very freedom to speak the foundational truth that God created the human race with two 'very good' genders, male and female, and they cannot be changed.

WAYNE GRUDEM
Distinguished Research Professor of Theology and Biblical Studies,
Phoenix Seminary, Phoenix, Arizona

# GENDER IDEOLOGY

## WHAT DO CHRISTIANS NEED TO KNOW?

SHARON JAMES

CHRISTIAN
FOCUS

Copyright © Sharon James 2019

paperback ISBN 978-1-5271-0481-5
epub ISBN 978-1-5271-0490-7
mobi ISBN 978-1-5271-0491-4

10 9 8 7 6 5 4 3 2

First published in 2019
Reprinted in 2020
by
Christian Focus Publications Ltd,
Geanies House, Fearn, Ross-shire,
IV20 1TW, Great Britain.

www.christianfocus.com

Cover by Pete Barnsley (CreativeHoot.com)

Printed in the USA

# Contents

Note: *The abbreviation **LGBT** throughout the book refers to Lesbian, Gay, Bisexual and Transgender.*

# Acknowledgements

Over the past number of years, I have spoken on this issue in many different meetings; and I'm grateful to all those who have raised helpful questions and offered their wisdom and advice. My thanks to all those who have read and commented on all or part of the book, especially Michael Taylor and John Denning. I am grateful to be able to work as part of the team at The Christian Institute. None of my writing would be possible without the unfailing encouragement of my husband Bill. The views expressed in this book are mine, and should not be taken to represent the views of any of the above. Any omissions or mistakes are likewise mine.

Sharon James
London, 2019

# Introduction
# Behind the 'Good News' stories –
# And why it matters to you

R yland Whittington was born in California in 2007. Her parents were thrilled to have a lovely, healthy little girl.[1]

But they claim that as soon as their daughter could talk, she said she wanted to be a boy. They concluded that she was 'transgender'. They cut her hair, dressed her as a boy, and always used masculine pronouns (such as 'he' and 'his'). When Ryland was only six, they took her to a huge Lesbian/Gay/Bisexual/Transgender 'diversity' event. The child was put up on the platform, where she told the audience:

> My name is Ryland Michael Whittington. I'm a transgender kid.
> I am six. I am a cool kid. I am the happiest I have ever been.[2]

---

1    Whittington, H, *Raising Ryland: Our Story of Parenting a Transgender Child with No Strings Attached*, William Morrow Paperbacks, 2016.

2    BBC Newsbeat online, 3 June 2014; see http://www.bbc.co.uk/newsbeat/article/27679841/i-am-six-and-im-a-transgender-kid-i-am-a-cool-kid (accessed 21 September 2018).

The media in the West usually presents such stories as 'good news'. We are supposed to respond: *That's wonderful. An unhappy little girl has been transformed into a happy little boy!*

In reality, such stories are evidence of deep confusion. Behind the 'good news stories' you sometimes see in the headlines, there are many people who once claimed to have 'changed sex' but discovered that it made their unhappiness worse. People like Walt Heyer.

## Walt Heyer's Story

Walt grew up in Los Angeles, California, during the 1940s. He often went to stay with his grandma at weekends. She liked to treat little Walt like a girl, dressing him up in pretty dresses. He loved the attention, and loved the way it felt to be dressed up as a girl.

> She lavished delighted praise upon me when I was dressed as a girl. Feelings of euphoria swept over me with her praise, followed later by depression and insecurity about being a boy. Her actions planted the idea in me that I was born in the wrong body.[3]

When his dad found this out, he began harshly disciplining his son, and didn't let him visit grandma without his parents again. Things got even worse when another older male relative began subjecting Walt to sexual abuse. Walt couldn't physically escape the violence, but in his imagination he created a place to escape. In that 'safe place', he imagined himself as a little girl, loved by grandma. These thoughts got so ingrained that his desire to be female never went away.

---

3    Heyer, W, 'I was a Transgender Woman', The Public Discourse, 14 April, 2015, http://www.thepublicdiscourse.com/2015/04/14688/ (accessed 21 September, 2018).

Walt achieved spectacular career success. He married and had children. But he never stopped wanting to be a woman. In his head, he associated being female with being safe and happy. He looked for comfort in drink, in hard work. Eventually he was advised that a 'sex change' would solve his problems. When he was forty-two, Walt had surgery and began taking female hormones. He now looked like a woman, and legally changed his name to Laura. He later wrote:

> I was generally happy for a while ... [But] Being a female turned out to be only a cover-up, not healing. I knew I wasn't a real woman, no matter what my identification documents said.[4]

Eventually, Christians reached out to him with love. Walt realised that while we can change appearance, we can't change what God created us to be. He made the difficult decision to go back to live as a man. Even though he had been physically mutilated, he wanted to stop 'living a lie'. He writes:

> Coming back to wholeness as a man after undergoing unnecessary gender surgery and living life legally and socially as a woman for years wasn't going to be easy. I had to admit to myself that going to a gender specialist when I first had issues had been a big mistake. I had to live with the reality that body parts were gone ... a sad consequence of using surgery to treat psychological illness ... But I had a firm foundation on which to begin my journey to restoration. I was living a life free from drugs and alcohol, and I was ready to become the man I was intended to be.[5]

---

4    Ibid.
5    Ibid.

Walt Heyer now runs a ministry to help those who end up regretting their so-called 'sex change' treatments.[6]

Of course, his is just one story. No story is the same. But here are lessons we can learn from his testimony:

## Gender confusion involves deep unhappiness

We should respond with compassion not hostility. Where there is confusion about gender identity, it is often a symptom, a warning sign, signalling deep anxieties arising from other factors. Many people (including children) suffering gender confusion are, effectively, victims of the false ideology of gender theory. We need to distinguish trans *activists* (those who are promoting this ideology) from people who are *suffering gender confusion*.

## We should treat everyone with kindness and respect

Christians treated Walt with kindness, but they cared for him too deeply to go along with the lie that he had really 'changed sex'.

## Real kindness means believing and telling the truth

After Walt started walking with the Lord, he came to realise that he needed to live out his created calling as a man, the man God had created him to be.

## We need to understand the ideas behind the claim that we can 'change sex'

If we are really to help people like Walt, we need to understand the ideology that led to him being told that he could 'change sex'.

## Why does this matter to you?

We live in an age of unprecedented confusion about sexual identity. Activists within international bodies such as the World

---

6    http://www.sexchangeregret.com/ (accessed 21 September, 2018).

Health Organisation, the United Nations, and the European Union have, for some time, been promoting 'gender theory', even in nations which are religiously and socially conservative. Gender theory says that we have a 'gender identity' which is independent of our biological sex. We may feel we are male, female, neither, or something else.

This matters to you, because these activists are getting this message out to children by means of 'comprehensive sexuality education'.[7] Wherever we live in the world, our children may be presented with a worldview that denies the truth that humans have been created as male or female.

You would think that the Christian Church would unite in protest against this new ideology.

Sadly, that is not the case. There are even professed Christians who are cheering it on. In 2007, former evangelical, Virginia Mollenkott wrote a book entitled *Omnigender: A Trans-Religious Approach*. She called for an omnigender future, where governments would no longer record people's sex; people could change their bodies at will; and all sports, prisons, and public toilets would be unisex.

Those who challenge the false claims of gender theory are accused of ignorance. Belief in basic human biology is thought to be 'transphobic'.[8] Parents who want to protect their children from this dangerous theory may find their children taken away from them. In February 2018, parents in Ohio were denied custody of their seventeen-year-old daughter when they refused to support

---

7    Kuby, G, *The Global Sexual Revolution: Destruction of Freedom in the Name of Freedom*, LifeSite, 2015, pp. 206-213.

8    For discussion of this term see chapter 3.

her desire to live as a boy and her request for cross-sex hormone treatment.[9]

This issue affects us all. This book aims to explain in simple terms what is going on.

There are other resources which give pastoral advice as to how to help gender-confused people. There are excellent books which examine in depth what the Bible says about sexual ethics. There are longer works which offer a more detailed critique of gender theory. This is not a fully documented academic treatise. If you want full documentation of the points made, recommended resources are listed at the end of this book.

I hope that by reading this introductory guide you will become more confident in the truth that we have been created male or female. My aim is that you will be better equipped to protect the next generation from believing lies that lead to lasting physical and emotional harm.

## Further reading

Walt Heyer, *Trans Life Survivors*, 2018.

---

9    'Parents lose custody of Child for Refusing to Support Transgenderism', *Daily Wire*, 19 February, 2018, https://www.dailywire.com/news/27309/parents-lose-custody-child-refusing-support-amanda-prestigiacomo (accessed 14 November, 2018).

# 1.
# The Global Sexual Revolution

W hen people look back to our era for iconic moments, one will be the 'coming out' of Bruce Jenner (b.1949) on the cover of *Vanity Fair* in July 2015. Posing as a glamour model, with the tag 'Call me Caitlyn', the world was told that although he'd been one of the all-time great American male Olympic heroes[1] and was now over sixty, he had 'always been a woman'. Bruce had not had reassignment surgery (that came two years later, in 2017). If you listen to Jenner today, he still has a man's voice. But history has been rewritten. On Father's Day 2018, Jenner's daughter Kylie posted a cute picture of herself as a little girl with her dad. The photograph was vilified as transphobic.[2]

This challenge to the man-woman blueprint, which lies at the foundation of family and society, is unprecedented.

By 2018, around twenty nations had passed laws affirming the 'right' to 'change sex' – nations including Argentina, Bolivia,

---

1    Bruce Jenner was the men's world record decathlon champion from August 10, 1975 – May 15, 1980.

2    https://www.foxnews.com/entertainment/kylie-jenners-fathers-day-tribute-to-caitlyn-jenner-called-transphobic (accessed 5 December 2018).

Colombia, Denmark, Ecuador, France, Iceland, Ireland, Japan, Malta, Norway, Spain, the United Kingdom, Uruguay and Vietnam.[3]

In such countries, a man can legally take a female name, and be treated for all legal purposes as a woman (or vice versa). He may be given a new birth certificate. In some of these countries, there is no requirement for such a person to undergo any medical treatment at all (such as hormonal treatment or surgical 'reassignment'). A physically normal man can demand to be recognised as a woman, and demand to freely access women-only facilities (such as swimming pool changing areas or public toilets).

Whether or not countries have passed such laws, powerful global organisations such as the International Planned Parenthood Federation (IPPF) and the United Nations Population Fund (UNFPA) want children in all countries to receive 'comprehensive

---

3    'Table of Gender Recognition Systems in Approved Countries and Territories Under the Gender Recognition Act 2004', HM Courts and Tribunals Services, 2011, http://hmctsformfinder.justice.gov.uk/HMCTS/GetLeaflet.do?court_leaflets_id=4521 (accessed 16 May 2017); 'Rights in Transition: Making Legal Recognition for Transgender People a Global Priority', Human Rights Watch, 2016, https://www.hrw.org/world-report/2016/rights-in-transition (accessed 16 May 2017); 'Bolivia Approves Progressive Law Recognising Transgender Rights', http://www.telesurtv.net/english/news/Bolivia-Approves-Progressive-Law-Recognizing-Transgender-Rights-20160521-0018.html (accessed 16 May 2017); 'Vietnam: Positive Step for Transgender Rights', Human Rights Watch, 30 November 2015, https://www.hrw.org/news/2015/11/30/vietnam-positive-step-transgender-rights (accessed 16 May 2017); 'Ecuadorean Lawmakers Approve New Gender Identity Bill', http://www.telesurtv.net/english/news/Ecuadorean-Lawmakers-Approve-New-Gender-Identity-Law-20151211-0001.html (accessed 16 May 2017); 'It's official – France adopts a new legal gender recognition procedure!' http://www.ilga-europe.org/resources/news/latest-news/france-adopts-new-legal-genderrecognition-procedure (accessed 16 May 2017).

sexuality education' (CSE).[4] This education programme tells children they have the *right* to express their own 'sexual orientation' and 'gender identity'. Over recent years, the United Nations has put pressure on member states to adopt this sexually permissive programme.

Many people assume that laws about 'gender recognition' are simply being passed in order to protect a tiny minority of troubled people from unfair discrimination. They think they can ignore what is going on, as it will only affect a very few. Some well-meaning people say that it's insensitive at best – and cruel at worst – to speak out strongly about this issue, as it will upset and offend these troubled people. That's why many people don't want to speak out openly against the promotion of transgender 'rights'.

But such laws affect us all.

And the more this ideology of gender theory takes hold, the more confusion is caused. It is true that many of the people who are most troubled are *not* deliberately setting out to promote this ideology. But they *are* victims of this ideology. And if we ignore the issue and remain silent, the number of these victims will only increase.

This ideology is summed up in a picture book written for four-year-old children called *The Gender Fairy*. It tells the children:

Only you know whether you are a boy or a girl. No one can tell you.[5]

The author of the book hopes that:

---

4    'Comprehensive sexuality education', United Nations Population Fund, see http://www.unfpa.org/comprehensive-sexuality-education (accessed 16 May 2017); 'Education', International Planned Parenthood Federation, see http://www.ippf.org/our-approach/services/education (accessed 16 May 2017); Kuby, G, *The Global Sexual Revolution: Destruction of Freedom in the Name of Freedom*, LifeSite, 2015, pp. 206-213.

5    Hurst, J, *The Gender Fairy*, Oban Road Publishing, 2015.

Some children will realize their true identity is not the gender they were assigned at birth, and will choose to make a social transition to live as their true gender. [6]

## Challenging the male-female distinction

The biological male/female distinction is the basis for the natural family of husband/wife and mother/father/children. Recognition of man-woman marriage has been foundational to human societies since the dawn of time. It is the best means of ensuring that children receive ongoing care from both their parents, and their wider extended family network. It is the building block of society, and the best provider of cross-generational support.

Gay rights activists object to calling man-woman marriage 'natural', because it implies that same-sex partnerships are 'unnatural'. They claim that it's *hateful* to believe that man-woman marriage is 'normal'. They want to cleanse societies across the globe of 'heteronormativity' (the idea that man-woman sexual relations are the norm).

The Gay, Lesbian, and Straight Educational Network (GLSEN) launched a 'Safe Space Kit' in 2009, aiming for it to be used in America's 100,000 middle and high schools. [7] GLSEN promotes a 'Homophobia Scale', defining homophobia as ranging from repulsion, pity, and tolerance to acceptance. The assumption here is that acceptance of homosexuality is still homophobia, because it's not positive enough. Correct attitudes, according to this thinking,

---

6    Hurst, J, The Gender Fairy, http://www.thegenderfairy.com/ (accessed 8 May 2017). Jo Hurst supported her six-year-old son to 'socially transition' (use a female name; wear female clothes; etc.)

7    Brown, M. L, *A Queer Thing Happened to America: And what a long, strange trip it's been*, EqualTime Books, 2011, p. 99.

*begin* with support, and then move up to admiration, appreciation, and (the best option,) nurture.[8]

In 2009, the *Quebec Policy against Homophobia* was published. The Government of Quebec was ruling that heterosexism must not be tolerated. How is 'heterosexism' defined? It is:

> Affirmation of heterosexuality as a social norm or the highest form of sexual orientation.[9]

So it's 'homophobic' to say that male-female sexual relations are the social norm (ie the natural means of human reproduction, and the sexual relations practised by the great majority of the sexually active population).

Some of those who aim to eliminate heterosexism want to go further – to get rid of the idea that it is normal to be either male or female. They denounce this biological truth as 'binary', 'oppressive', and 'cis-normative'. They want us to believe that a person with a penis can 'really' be a woman; and a person with a womb can 'really' be a man.

This is flying in the face of biological reality. It seems crazy to most adults in most cultures. The biological male/female distinction is hard-wired into nature. Yes, a tiny number of babies are occasionally born with a physical abnormality. In rare cases, their genitalia may be damaged or ambiguous. But in the past, this has always been regarded as being a physical disorder (just as other physical abnormalities are departures from the norm). Such cases have never before led people to deny that humanity is divided between men and women; boys and girls. The exceptional cases of intersex people have, effectively, been hijacked by activists – even though the majority of people who are genuinely intersex don't

---

8    Ibid, p. 117.

9    Ibid, p. 522.

want to be pulled into the campaign to promote radical gender ideology.[10]

Most adults instinctively know that the 'binary' division of humanity into male and female genders is an objective reality. But what about little children? They are highly impressionable, usually believing whatever adults tell them. If you can persuade them from an early age that they can identify as any gender, then – over time – recognition of the reality of fixed male/female distinctions will be weakened.

Our children are on the frontline. We need to understand *what* they are being taught. And we need to understand *why* this ideology is dangerous and wrong.

## Further Reading

Gabrielle Kuby, *The Global Sexual Revolution: Destruction of Freedom in the Name of Freedom*, LifeSite, 2015.

---

10  Intersex Society of North America, 'Why doesn't ISNA want to eradicate gender?' http://www.isna.org/faq/not_eradicating_gender (accessed 14 September, 2018).

# 2.
# 'Can we Really Change Sex?' and other FAQs

On 24 November 2018, a headline in the *New York Times* read:

My New Vagina Won't Make Me Happy

The author was born a boy, but is demanding surgical treatment to 'construct a vagina'. What will this achieve?

> Until the day I die, my body will regard the vagina as a wound; as a result it will require regular painful treatment to maintain. This is what I want, but there is no guarantee it will make me happier. In fact I don't expect it too. That should not disqualify me from getting it.[1]

In a world where millions of people lack basic health care, rich nations are spending money on 'constructing vaginas' for healthy men. What is going on?

---

1 Long Chu, A. 'My New Vagina Won't Make Me Happy: And It Shouldn't Have to', *New York Times*, 24 November, 2018, https://www.nytimes.com/2018/11/24/opinion/sunday/vaginoplasty-transgender-medicine.html (accessed 1 December 2018).

Before we jump into the strange new world of 'gender theory' (Chapter 3), we need to establish some definitions. To do that, we will look at ten of the most frequently asked questions.

## 1. What's the difference between 'sex' and 'gender'?

The word *sex* in English can be used in two senses. Firstly, it can refer to the *biological category* of male or female. If I am asked 'what sex are you?' I reply, 'I am a woman.'

Secondly, the word 'sex' in English can also refer to *sexual activity*, often being used specifically to refer to sexual intercourse.

The word *gender* comes from the Latin term for 'kind' or 'set'. That's why 'gender' is used for grammatical terms (in languages where pronouns and verb endings and so on vary according to whether they apply to a male or female). By the twentieth century, sociologists and anthropologists sometimes used the term 'gender roles' to describe the clothes worn, preferred occupations and so forth, of men and women in different societies. Across the thousands of different cultures in the world, there are, of course, many ways in which men and women live out their roles.

These variations in social role *do not* negate the reality of the existence of men and women. They *do not* mean there are more than two 'genders' (male and female). In the past, it was assumed that there would be a 'match' between biological sex (man/woman) and gender role (male/female). Unless you accept the claims of 'gender theory' (more about this soon!), the word *gender* can properly be used as a synonym for the first definition of sex. If asked 'what gender are you?' I would reply, 'I am a woman'.

But the term 'gender' has been hijacked by gender theorists.

Judith Butler, a lesbian feminist, pioneer of gender theory, and author of *Gender Trouble: Feminism and the Subversion of Identity* (1990), called for the dissolution of the 'binary' male/female structure of human existence. She called this 'the subversion of identity'. And *'gender'* became the magic word by which you could subvert identity. The word *'sex'* is definite and objective. The question 'What sex are you?' has two possible answers: man or woman. To shake up this basic certainty about human beings meant taking control of language. The word 'gender' was grabbed, and it has come to be used in infinitely malleable ways.

We look further at the concept of 'gender identity' in Chapter 3. We will see how this theory arose in Chapter 4. But, for now, be alert when you hear the slippery term 'gender'! The way it is often used *wrongly* implies that there can be a mismatch between your sex and your gender.

## 2. What does 'transgender' mean?

The umbrella term 'transgender' is often used to include everyone who feels *any* dissatisfaction with their biological sex, and also to those who want to 'cross-dress' (dress in the clothes of the opposite sex).

## 3. What about trans people, or transsexuals?

Transsexuals are people who are biologically normal and healthy men or women (not intersex) who live as members of the opposite sex (or who want to live as members of the opposite sex).

So a trans woman is a normal and healthy biological man. He believes that he has a female 'gender identity'. He wants to be recognised and accepted as a 'real woman'.

The key question is this: Is this trans woman (born male) *really* a man who is deluded into feeling that he is a woman? Or, on the other hand, is this trans woman *really* a woman who was 'born in the wrong (male) body'?

Trans people may or may not have undertaken hormonal and/ or surgical treatment to enable them to more convincingly appear as being a member of the opposite sex. Many of them would say that the physical aspects of their body are irrelevant to who they 'really' are. They may change their identity without any intention of undertaking medical or surgical treatment.

## 4. What is 'gender dysphoria'?

Gender 'dysphoria' means that a person is unhappy with their biological sex. They believe they would be more truly 'themselves' if they were able to live as a member of the opposite sex – or, in some cases, as neither male nor female (or as some chosen 'other' identity). This inner feeling is strong and persistent over time. It is sometimes described as 'feeling trapped in the wrong body'.

In the past, it had been understood that this is a psychological disorder. Until 2013, the *Diagnostic and Statistical Manual of Mental Disorders* (4th edition, 2000) used the term *'gender identity disorder'.* There are, of course, other cases where someone's feelings contradict the physical reality of their body. People with anorexia nervosa have a strong mental conviction that their body is fat, when it is not. That is a mental disorder. Or, there are people who have a form of body dysmorphia where they are convinced that a feature is ugly; and they engage in repeated plastic surgery to remedy a 'defect' that only they perceive. There are others who have a fixed desire to amputate a healthy limb. In such cases, you are justified in offering help to try to enable the sufferer to gain a true perception of their body.

But in this case, activists have rejected the implication that to feel discontent with one's biological sex is a 'disorder'. Cultural and political pressure – not scientific evidence – led to a change of terminology from 'disorder' to 'dysphoria'. The 5th edition of the *Diagnostic and Statistical Manual of Mental Disorders* (2013) says:

> Gender dysphoria refers to the distress that may accompany the incongruence between one's experienced or expressed gender and one's assigned gender.[2]

Using the word 'dysphoria' means that the distress suffered by someone with this condition can be explained by external social factors (such as lack of understanding and acceptance). Note, however, that it is still listed in the *Manual of Mental Disorders*.

If the term 'gender dysphoria' is used to describe a person's discontentment with their biological sex, then that is non-controversial. However, recent definitions of 'gender dysphoria' affirm the false notion of 'gender identity' as being something in conflict with biological sex (see Chapter 3).

In 2018, the World Health Organisation ruled that gender incongruence would be classified under sexual health issues, rather than mental disorders; and this was confirmed in 2019.[3] The group Transgender Europe announced:

> This is the result of tremendous effort by trans and gender diverse activists from around the world.[4]

Of course it was hailed as a victory: Gender incongruence is now regarded as being an identity to celebrate rather than being a condition to be treated. There's a huge contradiction, though.

---

2   *Fifth Edition of the Diagnostic and Statistical Manual of Mental Disorders*, 2013, p. 51.

3   https://www.bbc.co.uk/news/health-48448804 (accessed 3 July 2019).

4   Hale, J. L, 'The World Health Organisation Will no Longer Classify Gender Dysphoria as a Mental Illness', *Bustle*, 22 June, 2018, https://www.bustle.com/p/the-world-health-organization-will-no-longer-classify-gender-dysphoria-as-a-mental-illness-9557139 (accessed 1 December, 2018).

Gender activists are happy for gender incongruence to remain listed in the World Health Organisation International Classification of Diseases (ICD) so that access to 'necessary health interventions' such as hormone therapy and surgery can be demanded.[5]

## 5. Can gender dysphoria be treated?

When there is a 'mismatch' between body and mind, should you try to influence the mind to fit the body? Or do you try to re-shape the body to fit the mind? Should you be allowed to investigate the reasons behind that 'mismatch'? Such reasons may involve a whole range of factors relating to the past or present experience of the affected person. People who suffer from gender dysphoria often experience a range of mental health problems such as anxiety, depression, self-harm, suicidal desires, and also addictions (such as drugs or alcohol).

In the past, it was accepted that professional counsellors could seek to influence the mind to fit the body, and that they could try to address the variety of factors which contributed to gender confusion. It was recognised that it was essential to seek to diagnose, and then treat, underlying complex comorbid conditions. And then, treatment would consist of counselling designed to move the mind towards fitting the bodily reality. In some cases, among people who have suffered genuine gender dysphoria, this has helped them find peace with their body.

Until quite recently, leading Gender Identity Clinics were wary of 'self-declarations'. For example, a lead clinician at Charing Cross Gender Identity Clinic wrote in 2011:

The least certain diagnosis is that made by the patient, made as it is without any training or objectivity. This uncertainty is not lessened

5    Ibid.

by the patient's frequently high degree of conviction. Neither does the support of others with gender dysphoria help, since conviction leads people to associate with the like-minded and to discount or fail to seek out disharmonious views.[6]

As acceptance of gender theory has taken hold, professionals are increasingly expected to accept what the person presenting with gender dysphoria claims about themselves. It is then assumed that 'treatment' means supporting the person to socially transition to live as someone of the opposite sex; possible provision of cross-sex hormones; and possible 'reassignment surgery'. Increasingly, to say that transgender feelings are an indicator of a mental disorder is regarded as discrimination.[7] It becomes more and more problematic even to address other comorbid conditions. To offer any form of counselling to help a person's mind line up with their body is regarded as abuse. Counsellors who seek to address the mental and psychological issues (i.e. to move the mind to fit the body) are finding their right to practise challenged. There has been especially fierce debate about the appropriate treatment of children and adolescents presenting with gender dysphoria, and this is discussed in Chapter 6.

The question could be framed: 'Are professionals *allowed* to treat gender dysphoria?' In some countries they are *not* allowed to offer counselling to help the person embrace their true bodily identity. They *are* expected to accept what the troubled person

---

6   Dr James Barrett, quoted in Brunskell-Evans, H, and Moore, M, Eds., *Transgender Children and Young People: Born in Your Own Body*, Cambridge Scholars Publishing, 2018, p. 207.

7   'Memorandum of Understanding on Conversion Therapy in the UK', Version 2, October 2017, point 4. https://www.psychotherapy.org.uk/wp-content/uploads/2017/10/UKCP-Memorandum-of-Understanding-on-Conversion-Therapy-in-the-UK.pdf (accessed 23 May, 2019).

claims about their identity. They are expected to provide any 'treatments' that the person demands.

In 2017, a representative group of professionals and campaigning organisations in the UK wrote a statement committed to ending the practice of 'conversion therapy', which they defined as an umbrella term for:

> any model or individual viewpoint that demonstrates an assumption that any sexual orientation or gender identity is inherently preferable to any other, and which attempts to bring about a change of sexual orientation or gender identity.[8]

Sadly, some people of faith have gone beyond careful and biblical counselling into the realm of what is termed 'spiritual deliverance.' There are times where this has been attempted in ways that are insensitive, even damaging. These aberrations are sometimes cited by those who want to prohibit any counselling, even when a person troubled with transgender feelings really wants it. Such a person's right to seek help is denied.

## 6. What causes gender dysphoria?

Arguably, 'gender dysphoria' is too broad a description. Dr Michael Bailey and Dr Ray Blanchard suggest there are at least three distinct groups of people. Firstly, it includes young children presenting with gender dysphoria. Secondly, it includes those (mainly girls) who develop gender dysphoria in adolescence – a condition sometimes referred to as 'rapid-onset' gender dysphoria. Thirdly, it includes adolescent or adult natal males who experience a tendency to be sexually aroused by the thought of themselves being as female (this

---

8    Ibid, point 2.

is sometimes described as 'autogynephilia').[9] We will consider the first two groups (children and adolescents) in chapter 6.

It is not fully understood what causes these varying conditions. Some argue that there may be environmental factors, genetic factors, or issues to do with the upbringing and nurture of a child. In some cases, 'social contagion' – for example, the influence of peers or online groups – is a significant factor (we consider this in Chapter 6). It could be that a variety of factors contribute to gender confusion. Some argue that gender dysphoria means that someone has a 'female brain' in a male body. But a large-scale survey concluded that there's no reliable scientific evidence for this often-heard claim.[10]

## 7. How common is this condition?

True gender dysphoria is very rare. But it is very difficult to secure accurate statistics, as figures are often based simply on those seeking treatments in certain places at certain times.[11] However, the number of people (including children) who claim varying degrees of gender incongruence is rising rapidly (see Chapter 6). It is no accident that this increase has coincided with widespread promotion of gender theory.

---

9 Bailey, J. Michael, and Blanchard, Ray, 'Gender Dysphoria Is Not One Thing', *4thWaveNow*, 7 December, 2017, https://4thwavenow.com/2017/12/07/gender-dysphoria-is-not-one-thing/ (accessed 23 May, 2019).

10 Mayer L. S, and McHugh, P. R, eds., 'Sexuality and Gender: Findings from the Biological, Psychological, and Social Sciences', *The New Atlantis,* Special Report, No 50, Fall 2016, pp. 102-3.

11 For example, 'The DSM-5 estimates that between 0.005% to 0.014% of adult males and for adult natal females, from 0.002% to 0.003%. Since not all adults seeking hormone treatment and surgical reassignment attend speciality clinics, these rates are likely modest underestimates'.

## 8. What about 'intersex' people?

A tiny number of infants suffer from hormonal or genetic disorders which affect sexual development. When they are born, their external genitalia may be of ambiguous appearance. But such cases are rare: They comprise fewer than one out of every 5,000 births.[12] We need to see this in the medical context where, sadly, babies may be born with various development disorders. These people all need to be treated with compassion, and with as much medical skill as is available.

In unusual situations when it is genuinely difficult to tell if a baby is male or female, the kindest thing is to do what is necessary to facilitate necessary functioning such as the capacity to pass urine.[13] There will need to be a choice as to whether to bring the child up as a boy or girl (this is referred to as 'assigning gender'). It is wise not to undertake radical surgery – to align them with that assigned gender – too soon. As time passes, especially when puberty takes place, their true sex may become more apparent. The great majority of intersex people are happy to accept a gender assignment of male or female. They are not campaigning for a genderless society. They don't regard themselves as being a 'third gender class'.[14] Unless born with an intersex condition, a baby's identity as biologically male or female is apparent from their chromosomes; genitalia; etc.

---

12    Sax, L, 'How common is intersex?', Journal of Sex Research, 2002, https://www.ncbi.nlm.nih.gov/pubmed/12476264 (accessed 14 September, 2018).

13    Intersex Society of North America, 'What does ISNA recommend for children with intersex?' http://www.isna.org/faq/patient-centered (accessed 14 September 2018).

14    Intersex Society of North America, 'Why doesn't ISNA want to eradicate gender?' http://www.isna.org/faq/not_eradicating_gender (accessed 14 September, 2018).

These rare exceptions should not be used to cast doubt on God's creation design of male and female. The number of intersex babies is routinely inflated by campaigners and activists. It is conflated with conditions such as Klinefelter syndrome and Turner syndrome.

The sex of an individual is determined by a pair of sex chromosomes: female (XX), and male (XY). In a small number of cases, there may be one of the following chromosomal variations, but these do not place an individual on a spectrum of 'indeterminate biological sex'.

XXY = male

XXYY = male

XXX = female

X0 = female

In such cases, there may be some impairment of physical development and fertility, but the sex of the person is not in doubt.

## 9. What about those who refuse to identify as either sex?

Back in 2004, a journalist observed in the New York Times:

> Some transgender students aren't moving between sexes; they're parked somewhere in the middle and prefer to describe themselves as 'gender queer' – signifying that they reject the either-or male-female system.[15]

The promotion of gender theory has led to some people wanting to register a protest against what they claim is the 'injustice' of binary categories. They may cite the reality of rare intersex conditions as a justification for refusing to identify as either male or female. They are 'gender nonconformists'. These people may not

---

15  Bernstein, Fred A, 'On Campus, Rethinking Biology' , *New York Times,* 7 March 2004, https://www.nytimes.com/2004/03/07/style/on-campus-rethinking-biology-101.html (accessed 24 November, 2018).

necessarily be deeply conflicted about their identity. But, as 'gender nonconformists', they may claim the right to be 'gender fluid'. They want to identify however they want, and to change their identity whenever they want. Such people might support the 'Gender Free Coalition' (see Chapter 3). They are gender defiant. But they are not just defying gender. They are defying reality. It is unsurprising that the person who won the right to became the first legally 'non-binary' person in the US realised, within three years, that he had been deceived by gender theory, and went back to living in his birth sex (see chapter 3).

## 10. Can you change sex?

No. It is impossible to 'change sex'; you can only change appearance. Our birth sex cannot be changed.

But from the 1930s onwards, medical advances enabled doctors to 'treat' people who wanted to live as someone of the opposite sex by means of hormonal and surgical interventions.[16] It is possible, using hormone treatments and surgery, to transform a man into someone who looks like a woman and *vice versa*.

Advocates of gender theory prefer to speak of 'gender confirmation' surgery (rather than 'sex change surgery'). But whatever you call it, no amount of surgery can change a man into a woman, or a woman into a man. The xx or xy chromosomal pattern is set at conception. These chromosomes are found in nearly every cell of the body. A DNA test will always reveal who you truly are. Nothing can change our fundamental genetic make-up.

Surgeons can construct artificial genitalia. But recipients of these are not thereby able to play the reproductive role of the opposite sex: These artificial genitalia have no reproductive capacity.

---

16  Britain's first Gender Identity Clinic opened in London in 1966.

Of course, the claim of 'gender theory' is that biology is irrelevant – it's what we *feel* that matters. We turn to that claim in the next chapter.

## Further Reading

Lawrence, W, Mayer, LS, and Paul R McHugh, eds., 'Sexuality and Gender: Findings from the Biological, Psychological, and Social Sciences', *The New Atlantis*, Special Report, No. 50, Fall 2016.

# 3.
# What is 'Gender Theory'?

K ori Doty claims to be a 'non-binary genderqueer trans person'. When Kori had a baby, the child was given a gender neutral name (Searyl), and the sex question on the birth certificate was left blank. To enable access to health care, in 2017 Canadian authorities in British Columbia issued the infant with a health card with 'U' in the space where a child's sex is normally specified.[1]

That wasn't enough for Kori, who belongs to the Gender-Free Coalition.

'End State Assigned Gender!' they demand. 'The State has no business in the undies of the Nation', they claim.[2]

The group wants the removal of a gender/sex designation from all state-mandated documents – such as from birth certificates, passports, and driver's licences.

---

1   https://www.telegraph.co.uk/news/2017/07/03/canadian-baby-registered-gender-unspecified-possible-world-first/ (accessed 23 November, 2018). It is important for doctors to know a person's sex, as there are many implications for healthcare.

2   http://gender-freeidcoalition.ca/ (accessed 23 November, 2018).

Would that lead to liberation – or total confusion?

The answer to that question depends on whether or not you accept the claims of gender theory. And to understand what gender theory is, we need to go to an historical royal city on the island of Java in Indonesia: Yogyakarta.

## The Yogyakarta Principles: Teaching 'Traditional' Morality Classed as Discrimination

In 2007, a gathering of self-styled 'human rights experts' met in Yogyakarta, Indonesia.

They had no official authorization. They were activists for the LGBT cause, and they drew up a series of demands – ones which came to be known as the *Yogyakarta Principles*.

These demanded that human rights principles should be applied to all people, in every nation, whatever their *'sexual orientation'* or *'gender identity'*. A person's 'sexual orientation' was defined in a way that included any type of sexual preference. A person's 'gender identity' was defined as:

> Each person's deeply felt internal and individual experience of gender, which may or may not correspond to the sex assigned at birth.[3]

This was a demand that governments should accept that everyone has something called a 'gender identity' which may be *different* from their biological sex. The only definition of this was a 'deeply felt internal and individual experience'. Governments were told they should allow people to change their sexual identity if such people had a deeply felt desire to do so.

---

3    The Yogyakarta Principles, March 2007, page 6, see http://www.yogyakartaprinciples.org/principles-en/ (accessed 16 May 2017).

Was this simply an effort to make sure that minority groups should not be badly treated?

No. The *Yogyakarta Principles* represented a radical LGBT charter. If these principles were enshrined in law, it would mean that the following *ideas* would be regarded as being discrimination:

- *The belief that marriage is only between a man and a woman*
- *The belief that sexual activity should be restricted to marriage*
- *The belief that children have a right to know and be brought up by their own father and mother*
- *The belief that human beings are either male or female from birth*

Consider: These very *ideas* would be classed as discriminatory.

And this would mean that fundamental biblical teaching relating to God's creation design would be classed as discriminatory as well.

A small elite want to control how people across the world think. To achieve this, they aim to control how children and young people across the world are educated. Since 2007, the UN, the EU, and several national governments have committed to implementing these principles.[4] By doing so, they have pledged to embed *gender theory* into law and education.

## What is gender theory?

*The Genderbread Person* (see p. 41) is a cartoon figure commonly used to teach children and young people that each person is made up of different aspects of each gender:[5]

---

4    Kuby, G, *The Global Sexual Revolution: Destruction of Freedom in the Name of Freedom*, LifeSite, 2015, pp. 82-93.

5    https://www.genderbread.org/ This is, of course, an allusion to 'gingerbread man'. Since the sixteenth century, there have been records of baking cookies in the shape of a stylised person, flavoured with ginger; and they have been featured in folk tales and songs.

- *Sex* has to do with the body (genitals, chromosomes, hormones, body hair, and so on).
- *Gender Identity* has to do with your sense of self – who you, in your head, feel yourself to be.
- *Gender Expression* is how you present yourself to others. It has to do with your clothing, behaviour, actions, and ways of speaking.
- *Attraction.* This is to do with who you are romantically or physically (sexually) attracted to. Male? Female? Both? Other?

One LGBT group tells young people:

> Everyone has a gender identity. This is the gender that someone feels they are. This might be the same as the gender they were given as a baby, but it might not. They might feel like they are a different gender, or they might not feel like a boy or a girl.

## The False Claims of Gender Theory

*1. Binary is bad*
*2. Gender is a spectrum*
*3. Boy/girl; man/woman are just social constructs*
*4. We all have a 'gender identity' which may be different from our biological sex*

## 1. Binary is bad?

No! The human race is made up of male and female people. The word 'binary' simply means 'relating to two'. 'Binary' is the foundation of LGB and T!

Lesbians? They are women attracted to other women.

Gays? Men attracted to other men.

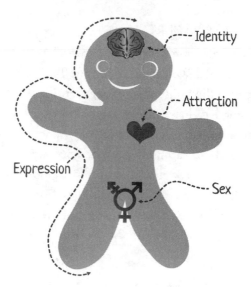

Identity

Attraction

Expression

Sex

*means a lack of what's on the right side*

Gender Identity

⊘——————→ Woman-ness
⊘——————→ Man-ness

Gender Expression

⊘——————→ Femininity
⊘——————→ Masculinity

Anatomical Sex

⊘——————→ Female-ness
⊘——————→ Male-ness

Identity ≠ Expression ≠ Sex
Gender ≠ Sexual Orientation

Sex Assigned At Birth
☐ Female ☐ Intersex ☐ Male

💜 Sexually Attracted to...      and/or (a/o)

⊘——————→ Women a/o Feminine a/o Female People
⊘——————→ Men a/o Masculine a/o Male People

💜 Romantically Attracted to...

⊘——————→ Women a/o Feminine a/o Female People
⊘——————→ Men a/o Masculine a/o Male People

Genderbread Person Version 4 created and uncopyrighted 2017 by Sam Killermann   For a bigger bite, read more at www.genderbread.org

Bisexuals? They are people attracted to both men and women. Trans people? They want to live as the 'other' of the two sexes. *All those categories are defined by 'binary' differences.*

## 2. Gender is a Spectrum?

There are an infinite number of ways in which we live out our lives as male and female. We are all different! But that doesn't mean there are seven billion different gender identities. It doesn't negate the fundamental reality that we are either men or women. The sheer absurdity of claiming that there is a spectrum of genders is seen in that in 2014, Facebook provided 56 ways that users could describe themselves (as well as male or female). But by 2018, it was felt that the list was incomplete, and 71 options were provided.[6] Most people won't have a clue what many of them mean. Neutrois? Androgyne? Two-spirit? No doubt the list will soon become even longer.

## 3. Boy/girl; man/woman are just social constructs?

No. They are universal human realities, not just socially constructed identities. The social roles lived out by men and women vary from place to place and from time to time. But sexual differentiation is a biological reality, not just a social construct.

## 4. Do we all have a 'gender identity' that may be separate from our sex?

The way men and women live (gender roles) varies from culture to culture. This does not mean that we can each claim a 'gender identity' that can be separated from our biological sex. A

---

6    Williams, R, 'Facebook's 71 gender options come to UK users', *Daily Telegraph*, 27 June, 2014, https://www.telegraph.co.uk/technology/ facebook/10930654/Facebooks-71-gender-options-come-to-UK-users. html (accessed 4 December, 2018).

comprehensive survey of the scientific evidence was published in 2016 in *The New Atlantis*. It discussed over 200 peer-reviewed studies in the biological, psychological, and social sciences – and concluded:

> The hypothesis that gender identity is an innate, fixed property of human beings that is independent of biological sex – that a person might be 'a man trapped in a woman's body' or 'a woman trapped in a man's body' – is not supported by scientific evidence.[7]

## Gender Theory has constructed a misleading vocabulary

In the absence of any scientific evidence, gender theory has gained acceptance by constructing a new vocabulary. If you control the language, you control the debate. We should be cautious about using the following words or phrases, except when we need to explain the views of others:

## 1. 'Assigned' at birth

This phrase is *only* correctly used in the case of infants who are born with a true intersex condition where their genitalia are of ambiguous appearance. Using this phrase for normal healthy children is ridiculous. It conjures up an image of a midwife maliciously and randomly putting a sinister label on an innocent infant. This phrase denies the reality of biology. It eliminates the importance of science. It tells us that the physical body is irrelevant to who we 'really' are as human beings. Philosopher Rebecca Reilly-Cooper comments:

---

7    Meyer, L. S, and McHugh, P. R, 'Sexuality and Gender: Findings from the Biological, Psychological, and Social Sciences', *The New Atlantis: A Journal of Technology & Society*, 50, Fall 2016, p. 8.

Correctly identifying the genitals that a child possesses and therefore the biological sex to which they belong is not a matter of 'assigning gender' to the child; it is simply to recognise the biological facts and to give them the correct biological label.[8]

## 2. 'Transphobia'

An anti-bullying charity defines 'transphobia' as follows:

Transphobia is intolerance of gender diversity. It is based around the idea that there are only two sexes - male or female - which you stay in from birth.[9]

Disagreement with gender theory is equated with 'intolerance' and 'phobia'. The implication is that disagreement is hateful, bigoted, and evil. Using the word 'transphobia' in this way is verbal bullying. It is possible to disagree with gender theory (i.e. believe that there are only two sexes which you stay in from birth) without being hateful or bigoted. Of course we should always abhor treating anyone with contempt or cruelty. There are laws in most countries against harassment or abuse. But there is no need for separate legalisation against 'transphobia': it just opens the door to intimidating people who don't agree with gender theory into compliance.

## 3. 'Cisgender'

This word is used to mean a 'non-transgendered person'. It is derived from the English preposition 'cis' meaning 'on the same side'. It implies that if a person has a mind that 'lines up' with

---

8    'Sex', Sex and Gender: A Beginner's Guide; see https://sexandgenderintro. com/ (accessed 20 September 2017).

9    Galop, 'What is Transphobia?' https://www.galop.org.uk/transphobia/ (accessed 16 November 2018).

their body, they are privileged. Using this term buys into the lie that there is a divide between our biological sex and our so-called 'gender identity'. Don't play this game. If asked 'Are you cisgender?', I would say, 'No, I'm not cisgender. I am a woman.'

## 4. 'Gender'

The word 'gender' has been hijacked.[10] Sex is a biological and bodily reality. Gender is the social expression of that physical reality. But the word 'gender' is often *misused* to imply that it can be *separated* from bodily reality. It can now mean anything you choose it to mean.

If someone asks 'what is your gender?' the accurate answer would be to give your biological sex. You are either a man or a woman. To be human is to be male or female. Every human is the product of the union of a man and a woman (even if their gametes have been artificially united in a laboratory). To be male or female is not about having particular body part/s that can be removed. It is written into the DNA of nearly every cell of your body.

## 5. 'Gender Neutral Pronouns' such as 'ze' and 'hir'

Here's how one trans support group explains what 'preferred gender pronouns' (PGPs) are:

> In English, the most commonly used singular gender neutral pronouns are ze (sometimes spelled zie) and hir. 'Ze' is the subject pronoun and is pronounced /zee/, and 'hir' is the object and possessive pronoun and is pronounced /heer/(hear). This is how they are used: 'Chris is the tallest person in class, and ze is also the

---

10   John Money (see chapter 4) used the word 'gender' in a paper about the treatment of intersex children in 1955; this seems to be the first academic article to use the word. Money believed that 'gender identity' in children is fluid. Meyer, L. S, and McHugh, P. R, 'Sexuality and Gender: Findings from the Biological, Psychological, and Social Sciences', p. 91.

fastest runner.' 'Tanzen is going to Hawaii over the break with hir parents. I'm so jealous of hir.'[11]

The guide goes on to explain that there are other PGPs, such as em/ier/eirs/eirself/emself; per/pers/perself; hu/hum/hus/humself and cheerfully says the list is 'ever-growing'. One might be tempted to laugh, but it's no laughing matter. In 2015, new civil rights guidelines were published in New York City, banning the 'misgendering' of individuals. If you insist on calling someone 'she' rather than 'ze', that could land you a $250,000 fine.[12]

## 'Gender theory' tells us to believe lies

Say you see a news headline, **'World's First Pregnant Man!'** Be discerning! It's *not a pregnant man* at all. It's a pregnant woman, who claims to be a man, and may have taken hormones so that she grows a beard.[13]

Or you see a news headline: **'Woman rapes fellow prisoners!'** Don't be taken in. *This is a violent man, who has claimed to be a woman*. He has not undergone sexual 'reassignment' surgery. Physically, he is no different to any other man, but he has been awarded a place in a female prison. He has assaulted fellow

---

11  'What the heck is a PGP?', Gay Straight Alliance for Safe Schools, https://www.gsafewi.org/wp-content/uploads/What-the-heck-is-a-PGP1.pdf (accessed 24 November, 2018).

12  'New York City will fine up to $250,000 for willful, malicious misuse of gender pronouns', LGBTQ Nation, 30 December 2015, https://www.lgbtqnation.com/2015/12/new-york-city-will-fine-up-to-250000-for-willful-malicious-misuse-of-gender-pronouns/ (accessed 7 June 2019).

13  Beatie, T, 'Labor of Love', The Advocate, 14 March, 2008, http://www.advocate.com/news/2008/03/14/labor-love (accessed 24 November, 2018); Meyer, L. S, and McHugh, P. R, 'Sexuality and Gender: Findings from the Biological, Psychological, and Social Sciences', p. 90.

inmates.[14] Of course, the women he has raped know full well that their attacker was a man. It is an insult to their suffering to deny it.

## Contradictions in gender theory

1. Gender theory holds that gender is *independent of biological sex*. It then expects that *biological sex may be altered* to 'fit' the individual's subjective sense of gender. Despite holding that gender is not the same as sex, it describes the medical recording of the true biological sex of a baby as 'assigning gender'.

2. Activists do *not want gender incongruence to be regarded as an 'illness'*. Rather, they regard it as an identity to be celebrated. They want people to be free to legally change identity without the 'intrusion' of a medical diagnosis (they want people to be able to self-declare or self-identify). But they also *demand costly medical interventions*, preferably paid for by other taxpayers or medical insurance schemes.

3. Gender theory celebrates each person's *freedom to live according to their felt gender identity*. But *freedom to 'de-transition' is disallowed*. Those who have gone through a 'sex change' and who have then regretted it are often intimidated into silence.

4. Some insist that *gender is 'fluid'*. However, undergoing *drastic alterations to one's body means there is no going back*.

5. The idea of *'gender fluidity'* is a direct contradiction of the idea of *'trans*gender', which involves a change of identity from one 'binary category' to the other.

---

14    Bannerman, L, and Lister, M, 'Rapist, Karen White, in women's jail "was trans-faker"', *The Times*, 10 September, 2018, https://www.thetimes.co.uk/article/rapist-karen-white-in-women-s-jail-was-trans-faker-lbcwjp8jc (accessed 24 November, 2018).

# Gender theory is a fraud – The testimony of James Shupe

In 2016, Jamie Shupe won the right to become the first legally non-binary person in the United States. Born in 1963, James had served with honour in the US Army for 18 years. He had married and had a daughter. He had retired from the army in 2000. But in 2013, James began living as a woman (Jamie), and persuaded the Army to change his sex to female on military records.

By 2016, he had realised that the reality was that his birth sex could not be altered. Equally, he could not reconcile that reality with what he experienced as 'feminine traits'. So he bought into the lie of gender theory. He became convinced that he was 'non binary'. He went to court, arguing:

> As a transgender person with male biology and distinctly feminine traits, I believe myself to be a unique variation of nature. I am not ashamed of who I am. I was not born into the wrong body. My genitals are not a birth defect. And I am not to be sterilized by psychiatry and a medical establishment that has run amok.[15]

Multnomah County Court, Oregon declared that he could change his sex designation to non-binary – the first legal recognition of a non-binary person in the US. After the court ruling, Jamie declared:

> After a historic court ruling, I am free. I am the first non-binary person in the United States to be officially recognized. I refused to be classified. And now, I've been vindicated. My court victory has broken a gender binary that many said could not be dismantled. In doing so, I have won the right to exist in any manner that I choose

---

15   Scupe, Jamie, 'I am the first official genderless person in the United States', *The Guardian*, 16 June, 2016, https://www.theguardian.com/commentisfree/2016/jun/16/i-am-first-official-genderless-person-united-states (accessed 30 May, 2019).

throughout the gender spectrum. The traditional constraints imposed by an unjust sex classification system of just male or female, that still governs those who lack my freedoms, has been lifted for me. In the face of adversity, I have declared my right to define my existence and won that right. But most importantly, my court victory has opened the door for all those like myself to also taste freedom from the gender binary.[16]

Jamie was issued with a birth certificate in Washington DC with the sex marker 'unknown'.

Within three years, Jamie realised that he'd been sold a lie. In 2019, he declared that gender theory is a fraud.

I believe that gender identity is a fraud perpetrated by psychiatry, the likes of something the United States and other nations hasn't experienced since the lobotomy era. As a result, I have returned to my male birth sex. In my thirty plus year marriage, I am the husband. To my daughter, I am her father. I no longer identify as a transgender or non-binary person and renounce all ties to transgenderism. I will not be a party to advancing harmful gender ideologies that are ruining lives, causing deaths and contributing to the sterilization and mutilation of gender-confused children. My history-making and landmark sex change to non-binary was a fraud based on the pseudoscience of gender identity. I am and have always been male. There should be no social or legal penalty for others to state that.[17]

Jamie went back to using his birth name James. But, like many others ('desisters' or 'regretters' or 'de-transitioners'), he soon found that social media and mainstream media didn't want to hear

---

16  Ibid.

17  Scupe, James, 'Public Announcement: I have Returned to my Male Birth Sex', https://jamieshupe.wordpress.com/category/announcements/ (accessed 30 May, 2019).

the truth. When he testified on Twitter that his gender dysphoria was a mental illness, he was 'blocked' for 'violating the rules against hateful conduct'. (He then noted that in just two years, the 994 active service military personnel diagnosed with gender dysphoria accounted for 30,000 mental health visits, asking 'how can it be a Twitter hate crime to say Gender Dysphoria is a mental illness?')

James Shupe is a living testimony to the fact that gender theory is a fraudulent, deceptive, and destructive lie.

## Gender Theory is a Lie

Firstly, gender theory is a *denial of basic biology*. In 2017, a group of those who were concerned about the promotion of gender theory to school children in Spain sent a 'bus of freedom' to drive around leading Spanish cities to alert parents to what their children were being taught. The message emblazoned down each side of the bus was a statement of fact:

*Boys have penises. Girls have vulvas. Don't be fooled.*

LGBT activists launched protests. They said that proclaiming this biological fact was 'transphobic'. City authorities in Barcelona, Pamplona, and Madrid were forced to ban the bus.[18] Children in Spain will continue to be taught a lie: that girls can have penises and boys can have vulvas.

Secondly, gender theory *destroys the definition of men, women; mothers and fathers*. If the only condition for 'being a woman' is to 'feel like a woman', then the question 'what is a woman' has to be answered: 'a person who feels like a woman'. That is a circular

---

18    White, L, 'They are Coming for Your children – the rise of Citizen-Go', *50.50: Gender, Sexuality and Justice*, 9 August 2017, https://www.opendemocracy.net/5050/lara-whyte/the-rise-of-citizengo (accessed 24 November 2018).

definition which says precisely nothing about what a woman is. It is an insult to women. The British Medical Association has advised staff not to refer to pregnant women as 'expectant mothers', in case that offends transgender people. ('Call them pregnant people' the BMA suggests).[19] So the category of 'mother' is eliminated.

Thirdly, gender theory leads to a *denial of history*. The 2004 Gender Recognition Act in the United Kingdom stated that when a person has lived for two years 'as someone of the opposite sex', they can apply for a gender recognition certificate.[20] They do not need to have undergone 'reassignment surgery' or taken any cross-sex hormones. But if they are given the gender recognition certificate, they can also be issued with a new birth certificate. Rewriting a birth certificate is state-sanctioned lying. In any other context, to go back and rewrite historical documents is rightly considered fraud.

Gender theory is a lie. Yet in many countries, people are being intimidated into going along with this lie. They are accused of 'transphobia', 'hate crimes', or 'discrimination' if they refuse. We turn in the next chapter to examine *how* these false claims of gender theory have arisen.

---

19  Donnelly, L, 'Don't call pregnant women "expectant mothers" as it might offend transgender people, BMA says', *Daily Telegraph*, 29 January, 2017, https://www.telegraph.co.uk/news/2017/01/29/dont-call-preg-nant-women-expectant-mothers-might-offend-transgender/ (accessed 24 November, 2018).

20  As of early 2019, the British Government was consulting on removing the need to live in the preferred gender for two years before applying for a gender recognition certificate. It was proposed to move to a policy of 'gender self-ID', which would require little more than signing a statement, and no medical oversight or treatment, for anyone to obtain a legal gender change. Just eight years earlier, in 2011, psychiatrists at leading Gender Identity Clinics warned of the dangers of 'self-definition'. But now, there is demand to legalise it. Transgender Children and Young People: Born in your Own Body, p. 207.

# Further Reading

Ryan Anderson, *When Harry Became Sally: Responding to the Transgender Moment*, Encounter Books, 2018.

# 4.
# Where did 'Gender Theory' come from?

In 2017, a law was passed in California against care providers in care homes who use the 'wrong' pronoun or name for residents who claim to have changed sex. Such care providers can be imprisoned for up to a year for the crime of 'misgendering'.[1] The state of California is enforcing acceptance of gender theory, and tolerating no dissent.

But it's only theory, and a relatively new theory at that. There is *no scientific evidence* to back up the idea that we all have a 'gender identity' that can be separated from our biological sex.[2]

Gender theory is an attack on the idea that we have a fixed sexual identity. It is an attack on the belief that there is anything normal about the division of humanity into male and female.

---

1    Hagstrom, A, 'California can now jail people for misusing gender pronouns', Daily Caller, 6 October 2017, http://dailycaller.com/2017/10/06/california-can-now-jail-people-for-misusing-gender-pronouns/ (accessed 11 October 2017).

2    Meyer, L. S, and McHugh, P. R, 'Sexuality and Gender: Findings from the Biological, Psychological, and Social Sciences', *The New Atlantis: A Journal of Technology & Society*, 50, Fall 2016, p. 8.

Those who have lived through the sexual revolution in Western culture, and have imbibed its teachings, assume that everyone has the right to fulfil themselves sexually just as they please. Whatever their desires, they can claim that is their 'orientation'. The concept of 'orientation' is relatively recent; a linguistic device which conveys the idea that some behaviours are due to fixed inborn identity. But there is no scientific evidence to support this concept.[3]

Gender theory pushes this further. You don't just have a right to live according to your 'sexual orientation' (regarding whom you desire to have sexual relations *with*). You also have the right to live in keeping with your 'deeply felt gender identity', whatever that is, and whether or not it is in keeping with your biological sex. In other words, you claim the right to decide who you have sexual relations *as*.

To challenge the human reality of the male-female distinction is revolutionary. Where did this idea come from? Some readers may prefer to skip the rest of this chapter and go straight on to look at God's good design in Chapter 5. But to fully understand gender theory, it is useful to see how it arose from the convergence of the sexual revolution and the cultural revolution. Behind these radical and destructive movements lurked the malevolent philosophy of Friedrich Nietzsche (1844-1900). His philosophy was based on the premise that God is dead. The logical outcome? No objective truth. No absolute morals. Nietzsche demanded that repressive Christianity must give way to unlimited freedom. The following key thinkers all picked up on that theme of liberation.

---

3    Ibid, pp. 13-58. The Executive Summary on p. 7 concludes: 'The understanding of sexual orientation as an innate, biologically fixed property of human beings – that people are "born that way" – is not supported by scientific evidence.'

## Eight Pioneers of Sexual Revolution

### 1. Karl Ulrichs (1825–1895)

Karl Heinrich Ulrichs was a nineteenth century German doctor, and campaigner for homosexual rights. He advanced the theory of a *female soul in a man's body* in order to argue the case that homosexuality was innate and should not be penalised. At this time, homosexuals were thought to experience 'sexual inversion'. Male 'inverts' were thought to have a *feminine soul in a male body*. This was the beginning of the idea that biological sex could be *divided* from the gendered experience.

### 2. Sigmund Freud (1856–1939)

Sigmund Freud, an Austrian neurologist and author, was the founder of psychoanalysis. He regarded religion as an illusion, a purely human construct. He thought the idea of a God was a fairy story, based on the infant's need for a father-figure. He believed that human suffering was caused by religion. Freud taught that guilt feelings were an illusion to be dispelled. Conscience was a force to be subdued. We have to get rid of shame. Freud regarded humans as just highly developed animals, and he regarded sexual desire in purely physical terms. He believed that children, from the earliest age, have sexual desires; and he rejected the notion of childish innocence. And he saw the family as the seedbed of neuroses and other disorders. Freud's 'achievement' was to construct a whole understanding of sexuality that was empty of moral criteria: 'the gateway to the sexual revolution was now opened wide'.[4]

---

4    Williams, E. S, *Lessons in Depravity*, Belmont House Publishing, 2003, p. 62.

## 3. Magnus Hirschfeld (1868-1935)

Hirschfeld, sometimes called the architect of the sexual revolution, was a gay doctor and activist. He believed that every man and woman is a mixture of male and female characteristics, and he devised a classification of 'gender variant' individuals in 1910. He worked with Dr. Eugen Steinach who performed experiments on animals, transplanting male and female reproductive glands. Understanding of male and female hormones advanced after Hirschfeld founded the Institute for Sexual Science in Berlin in 1919. Hirschfeld later oversaw the first 'sex reassignment' surgeries, including the series of operations performed on Einar Wegener, who went on to live as Lili Elbe, and whose story was told in the 2015 film 'The Danish Girl'. (Wegener was probably intersex, and he died following his fifth operation). Hirschfeld delivered the first scientific lecture on 'transsexualism' in 1930.

## 4. Alfred Kinsey (1894-1956)

Alfred Kinsey, a twentieth century sexual researcher, was addicted to sexual perversion. He claimed that from infancy, children were sexually active and should be encouraged to satisfy their desires. His 'experiments' involved the abuse of infants and children.[5] Kinsey aimed for the overthrow of all legislation which restricted sexual freedom. *The Kinsey Reports* were published under the titles *Sexual behaviour in the human male* (1948) and *Sexual behaviour in the human female* (1953). These deceived the American public into thinking that it was normal to engage homosexual behaviour, to use pornography, and much else. Kinsey claimed:

---

5    Ibid, pp. 80-84, 90-91.

Unless we want to close our eyes to the truth or imprison 95% of our male population, we must completely revise our legal and moral codes.[6]

For Kinsey, nothing was unnatural if people wanted to do it – including bestiality.[7]

## 5. Harry Benjamin (1885–1986)

Kinsey's associate, Harry Benjamin, wrote the first textbook on transsexualism in 1966. This book argued that the logical outcome of accepting evolution was also accepting gender fluidity. It looked to a future where scientific and medical advances would make it possible to change a biological male into a woman with full capacity to reproduce (as a woman):

Darwin's theory has pointed up the identity of male and female origins. Out of the same basic living molecules there were evolved different sex patterns, male and female. Thus the old language of opposite sexes, derived from the theological mythology that God (male) created male and female as absolutely separate creatures, has been modified by modern biology. Out of the same molecules the chemist can produce estrogens and androgens ... Out of the same nucleic acids the chromosomes that make a man or a woman are evolved. Medical arts can bring about the dramatic womanization of a man, or manization of a woman ... the progress of medical science and technology, I believe, will eventually make it possible to change a normal man into a normal woman with the capacity to become a reproducing other.[8]

---

6   Kuby, G, *The Global Sexual Revolution: Destruction of Freedom in the Name of Freedom*, LifeSite, 2015, p. 32.

7   Williams, E. S, *Lessons in Depravity*, pp. 89-90.

8   Benjamin, H, *The Transsexual Phenomenon*, The Julian Press, New York, 1966. Appendix B: 'Complementarity of the Sexes', by Gobind Behan Lal.

Benjamin pioneered the idea that if someone was convinced they were living in the wrong body, then the body should be fixed to fit with what their mind said, rather than attempting to change their mind to fit the biological facts. He provided patients with hormone treatment, and recruited other medical colleagues to assist with surgery and other treatments. Like Alfred Kinsey, Harry Benjamin advocated paedophilia. They both endorsed a book by their friend Rene Guyon, *The Ethics of Sexual Acts* (1948), which advocated decriminalising sex with children.

## 6. Wilhelm Reich (1897-1957)

Reich was an Austrian doctor of medicine and also a psychoanalyst. He believed that the suffering and cruelty in society were due to the enforcement of Christian morality. Traditional marriage, he argued, wrongly deprived women and children of their sexual rights. Like Freud, he wanted to liberate people from shame. Also like Freud, he promoted the idea that children should be able to engage in sexual activity. Sexual suppression in childhood, he said, led to unhappiness throughout life. In *The Mass Psychology of Fascism* (1933), he argued that fascism arose because people had suffered sexual repression. Reich suffered abuse himself as a child, and inflicted sexual abuse on young patients. He promoted permissive sex education as the way by which children could be liberated from oppressive moral codes.[9]

## 7. John Money (1921-2006)

One of Harry Benjamin's colleagues was the psychiatry professor, John Money. Like Kinsey and Benjamin, Money campaigned for the freedom to 'change gender'. (Also like Kinsey and Benjamin,

---

9    Williams, E. S, *Lessons in Depravity*, pp. 98-101.

Money advocated decriminalising sex with children.)[10] Money was the co-founder of the Johns Hopkins Gender Identity Clinic. He hit the headlines in America in 1966 with a groundbreaking case of a 'man who'd become a woman'.[11]

His most famous alleged success story related to a little boy, David Reimer, whose circumcision had gone wrong. Money advised David's parents to agree to experimental surgery to 'change' the little boy into a little girl. Money wanted to test his idea that gender is about socialisation not biology. If this boy could be brought up successfully as a girl, while his twin brother Brian was brought up as a boy, it would vindicate his theory. It was later revealed that Money had forced David (who was brought up as 'Brenda') to engage in incestuous acts with his brother. Over the years, Money had effectively sexually abused these two youngsters. He ruined their lives. When he was a teenager, David found out the truth about what had happened to him as an infant, and insisted on reverting to live in his true sex. Given the trauma they had gone through, it is not surprising that Brian died of a drug overdose aged thirty-six, and David committed suicide, aged thirty-eight.[12] This was a particularly tragic example of the harm done by professionals thinking they can intervene to change a child's gender identity.

---

10    Heyer, W, *Paper Genders: Pulling the Mask Off the Transgender Phenomenon*, Make Waves Publishing, 2011, pp. 7-8.

11    Ibid, pp. 8-9.

12    van Gend, D, *Stealing from a Child: The Injustice of 'Marriage Equality'*, Connor Court Publishing, 2016, pages 152-153; '"Sex-Change" Surgery: What Bruce Jenner, Dianne Sawyer and You Should Know', *Public Discourse*, 27 April 2015. See http://www.thepublicdiscourse.com/2015/04/14905/ (accessed 12 May 2017).

## 8. Robert Stoller (1924-1991)

Robert J. Stoller argued that sex is biological (what we are born as), and gender is social (what we learn through socialisation). He presented these ideas in *Sex and Gender* (1968). He also distinguished gender *identity* (personal awareness of belonging to one sex and not the other) from gender *role* (the behaviour one displays in society). He challenged the idea that one can distinguish between normal and perverted sexual behaviour. For him, the only significant boundary is whether any form of sexual behaviour infringes on other people's rights.

## What about the evidence?

The transsexual cause underwent a setback during the 1970s. Professor Paul McHugh had been the senior psychiatrist at Johns Hopkins Gender Identity Clinic. Along with Dr Meyer, he conducted a survey of 50 transsexuals who had been treated there. He explained that those who had undergone 'sex reassignment' surgery were little improved in their psychological condition afterwards, and concluded:

> Hopkins was fundamentally cooperating with a mental illness. We psychiatrists, I thought, would do better to concentrate on trying to fix their minds and not their genitals.[13]

The Johns Hopkins Gender Identity Clinic stopped performing 'sex reassignment' operations, as did many university-based gender

---

13 'Surgical Sex: Why we stopped doing sex change operations', *First Things*, November 2004, https://www.firstthings.com/article/2004/11/surgical-sex (accessed 12 May 2017); 'Hopkins Hospital: a history of sex reassignment', *The Johns Hopkins News-Letter*, 1 May 2014, http://www.jhunewsletter.com/2014/05/01/hopkins-hospital-a-history-of-sex-reassignment-76004/ (accessed 16 May 2017).

clinics; but surgeons continued to perform these operations elsewhere.

Despite evidence that these attempts to reassign people were not delivering lasting happiness, the assault on the fundamental man-woman distinction didn't stop. By this time, those suffering gender confusion had been claimed as being the most oppressed of the 'victim classes' by representatives of another powerful revolution, a cultural revolution sometimes described as 'Cultural Marxism', sometimes referred to as 'Critical Theory'.

## Pioneers of Cultural Revolution

One of the most destructive and evil movements in history was unleashed when Karl Marx (1818-1883) demanded the abolition of private property in the name of liberating the world's poor. Communist regimes around the world were responsible for the deaths of around 110 million people from 1900 to 1987.[14] *Economic* Marxism may have been discredited. But the narrative of oppression has been carried over into a powerful force – cultural Marxism (critical theory) – which views all reality through the lens of 'Who holds power?'[15] By looking at two of the pioneers of this movement, we will see how critical theory converged with the sexual revolution to produce the current dogma of identity politics.

---

14   Rummel, R. J, *Death By Government*, 1994, p. 15, Table 1.6.

15   For more on this, see Tinker, M, *That Hideous Strength: How the West was Lost, the Cancer of Cultural Marxism in the Church, The World, and the Gospel of Change*, Evangelical Press, 2018; and Shenvi, Neil and Sawyer, Pat, 'The Incompatibility of Critical Theory and Christianity', The Gospel Coalition, May 15, 2019, https://www.thegospelcoalition.org/article/incompatibility-critical-theory-christianity/ (accessed 24 May, 2019).

## 1. Antonio Gramsci (1891–1937)

The Italian Marxist Antonio Gramsci distanced himself from aspects of economic Marxism, but reworked Marxism as an ongoing demand for human liberation. He maintained that people are to be set free; and that the instruments of oppression are institutions like the family and the church. His theory of 'cultural hegemony' describes how the state and the ruling capitalist class holds power (the Greek word *hegemon* means ruler). The ruling class keeps power by enforcing values and norms (such as traditional morality). Those values and norms (such as those promoted by Christianity) must be overthrown. But you don't frighten people by calling this process 'neo-Marxism'. You use the language of equality and freedom.

## 2 Herbert Marcuse (1898–1979)

Marcuse was a philosopher and sociologist associated with the Frankfurt School (or Institute for Social Research). This was a Marxist study centre, founded in 1923, which sought to destabilise capitalist societies by means of 'critical theory'. The 'long march' through key institutions (including educational, media, corporate, and religious bodies) would commence: infiltrating them with persistent challenges to all conventional values. Any who questioned this could be smeared with labels such as bourgeois, superstitious, authoritarian, or fascist. (Christians, of course, were labelled 'all the above').

Marcuse shot to international fame in 1955 with the publication of *Eros and Civilisation*. In this book, he brought together the ideas of Marx and Freud in order to demand a non-repressive society (a society liberated from traditional moral norms). Freud had described (what he regarded as being) the 'sexual desires' of infants as being as undifferentiated (focused on any part of the body, and likely to be bi-sexual or incestuous).[16] He had called this 'polymorphous perversity'. Later on, the child's raw desire would be constrained by education into social norms. *Marcuse* advocated unravelling those social norms – liberating adults back into that joyous freedom of polymorphous perversity. Throw out restraints. Any behaviour is acceptable.

Marcuse argued that in a free society, tolerance of different lifestyles would be exposed for what it really is: a pseudo-tolerance which assumed the repressive superstructure of traditional norms. He called this 'repressive tolerance' and said that it must not be tolerated! So, the new tolerance could justify eliminating the old tolerance. This is the pretext by which you can get rid of any who still believe in absolute moral standards. This is the justification for censoring those who advocate such 'repressive ideas' as marital fidelity or heteronormativity or childhood innocence. The flip side of complete freedom is murderous intolerance.

Herbert Marcuse has been described as the father of the new left and of the student protest movements of the 1960s. His lasting and destructive legacy was the unravelling of any confidence in truth. He aimed to break the established universe of meaning. That would be achieved if you could persuade a gullible population of students that words don't actually 'mean' anything – they are just 'tools' to achieve what the writer or speaker wants. This was the project of deconstruction, *aka* (also known as) the project of cultural subversion. It is most often referred to today as 'critical theory'. It has been stunningly successful.

In view of that success, it is no longer quite so surprising that grown-ups and seemingly intelligent people can say with a straight face that girls can be boys, and boys can be girls.

---

16   The idea that infants have sexual desires is utter perversion.

## The advent of identity politics

Once you've abolished truth, you are left in a society where value and worth are assigned to people on the basis of their place in a hierarchy of power. Those at the top of the hierarchy are the privileged oppressors (such as white, educated, 'cisgender', able-bodied males). Those at the bottom are the oppressed victims (such as people of colour, disabled, trans, and uneducated people). Welcome to the brave new world of identity politics!

In this inverted universe, those at the 'top' are stripped of their right to make any comment on the position of those at the 'bottom'. Those with privilege are not qualified to comment on the situation of those without privilege – and are not allowed to question their claims or to challenge their demands.

The trump card is played when you invoke 'intersectionality' to show how someone can suffer layers of oppression. If someone is marginalised due to multiple factors: racism, sexism, homophobia, transphobia, and so on, then their victim status is assured. Those who are enlightened about the plight of the victim class/es are sometimes described as 'woke' (i.e. 'aware').

Those classified as being 'without privilege', or as being 'victims', can claim at any time to have been offended, distressed, or insulted, no matter whether there's any objective ground for their claim. It is their perception that matters. Such feelings are subjective, but they cannot be challenged. Someone might claim offence from hearing a sermon. Distress from reading a Bible text. Insult from receiving an invitation to a carol service. They can demand that a visiting lecturer be banned from a campus, or that a university group be disaffiliated. Trauma might be 'triggered' if they hear any expression of a different view from their own.

The triumph of identity politics is why people suffering gender confusion are often presented as the heroes of our time. In 2014, the celebrated star of the Netflix drama *Orange Is the New Black*, Laverne Cox, appeared on the front page of TIME magazine in his chosen female identity. Cox was born a boy. TIME had only admiration and praise for this person's courageous and heroic journey to live out his 'real' identity.

## The convergence of Identity Politics, Radical Feminism, and Queer Theory

The first wave of feminism had focused on campaigning for equal rights for women. During the 1960s, some second wave, or radical, feminists argued that to maintain *any* gender distinctions propped up the edifice of oppressive 'patriarchy'.[17] Some said that to affirm any essential differences between the sexes was the 'heresy' of 'essentialism'. Judith Lorber, a radical feminist, wrote:

> When we no longer ask 'boy or girl?' in order to start gendering an infant, when the information is as irrelevant as the colour of a child's eyes … only then will men and women be socially interchangeable and really equal. And when that happens there will no longer be any need for gender at all.[18]

At the same time, those campaigning for gay rights asserted that the assumption that heterosexuality is 'normal' is hateful, and asserted the belief that heterosexual marriage is foundational to societal stability is oppressive. The theory underpinning this became known as 'queer theory'. The term was deliberately provocative, seeking to gain attention. The aim was to challenge the belief that

---

17    For a more detailed discussion of feminism, see James, S. *God's Design for Women in an Age of Gender Confusion*, Evangelical Press, 2019.

18    Quoted in Germaine Greer, *The Whole Woman*, Doubleday, London, 1999, p. 324.

man-woman sexual relations are normal. Such a belief was labelled 'heteronormativity' and was regarded as hateful.

The alliance of cultural Marxism (or critical theory) with Queer Theory resulted in sexual minorities being regarded as being the most victimised of the victim classes. Their claims could not be gainsaid – any criticism was automatically classified as coming from 'a position of privilege' and was therefore seen as being able to be automatically discounted.

Judith Butler, author of *Gender Trouble: Feminism and the Subversion of Identity* (1990), argued that the 'binary' framework for both sex and gender is just a fiction – made up by the oppressive class of heterosexual males, in order to maintain their advantage.[19] She advanced the idea that being a man or a woman is not something that we are, but that rather, it is something we *do* (a 'performance'). Someone with a female body may 'perform socially' as a male – and in that case the word 'man' can be used to signify a female body. One can see why she called this the 'subversion of identity'. Butler and others argued that not only is *gender* a social construct, *sexual differentiation* itself need not be fixed. If our sexual orientation (who we are attracted to) is fluid (i.e., whether we are sexually attracted to those of our own sex or to those of the opposite sex), why not our sexual identity (who we see ourselves as being) as well?

During the 1980s and 1990s, a new collective identity emerged – of Lesbian, Gay, Bisexual and Trans (LGBT) people. In time, more letters would be added so as to include those who identified as queer (Q), intersex people (I), those who claim to be 'asexual' (attracted neither to male or female, (A) and anyone else (+). The acronym now looks like this: LGBTQIA+.

---

19   Butler, Judith, *Gender Trouble: Feminism and the Subversion of Identity*, Routledge, 1990/1999, p. 44.

Queer theory takes the moral high ground. It is thought to be abusive to 'assign' people to one sex. It is thought to be hateful not to allow people to choose (or 'recognise') their own unique identity. Most people would not be interested in queer theory. But the notion of gender fluidity has permeated our culture with astonishing speed. To challenge it, is often regarded as being bigoted.

## The Threat to Freedom

Insisting on the legal right to live in any 'gender identity' means that someone's personal feelings must be respected, even when those feelings contradict biological facts. They can demand that you call them by a name (and pronouns) that contradict physical reality. That's why the state of California decided to penalise care providers who refused to address people in care homes by their preferred names and pronouns.

That's the reason why an elite women's college in America, Wellesley College, introduced a new admission policy. They will admit (biological) *men* who claim to be *women*. They will not admit (biological) *women* who claim to be *men*.[20] The assumption behind this admission policy? 'Gender' is all in the mind. We can define ourselves. The claim to be able to 'define ourselves' is the logical outworking of the hyper-individualism of Western societies. Each individual is to be free and self-determining, not constrained by social expectations regarding gender.

Despite a lack of any scientific grounding, gender theory has become mainstream. It is being integrated into the legal and educational systems in a number of countries. And in some countries, there are laws to silence any opposition to this theory.

---

20 Wellesley College Admission Policy, FAQs, https://www.wellesley.edu/admission/faq#transgender (accessed 6 March 2016).

In Canada, Bill C-16 became law in June 2017. It adds 'gender identity and gender expression' to the list of prohibited grounds of discrimination. That means that any questioning of a person's claims to identify as the opposite sex can be classed as hate speech.[21] Penalties could be exacted from any who 'mis-gender' others, or who refuse to use gender-neutral pronouns. This poses an unprecedented challenge to freedom of speech and expression. It places subjective feeling over scientific fact. The passing of Bill C-16 was firmly opposed by the academic Jordan Peterson of Toronto University. He believes that the Bill enforces linguistic untruth. Peterson argues that terms like 'gender identity' are the 'propositions of radical social constructionists', and are being used to bully opponents into submission. He sees – with moral clarity – the threat cultural Marxism (or critical theory) and gender theory pose to human freedom.[22]

And all this poses a direct challenge to religious freedom. It threatens to silence churches and parents who seek to teach the biblical truth that 'male and female He created them'. We turn in Chapter 5 to look at that good design.

## Further Reading

Walt Heyer, *Paper Genders: Pulling the Mask Off the Transgender Phenomenon*, Make Waves, 2011.

Melvin Tinker, *That Hideous Strength, How the West was Lost: The cancer of Cultural Marxism in the church, the world and the Gospel of Change*, Evangelical Press, 2018.

---

21 Jordan B. Peterson, 'Fear and the Law', 27 September 2016, https://youtube/fvPgjg201w0 (accessed 12 May 2017).

22 'Toronto Professor Jordan Peterson takes on gender-neutral pronouns', BBC News, Toronto, 4 November, 2016, http://www.bbc.co.uk/news/world-us-canada-37875695 (accessed 21 September 2017).

# 5.
# Male and Female – by Design

ore than 73 million people worldwide watched the American crime series CSI (Crime Scene Investigation) during 2009. Such programmes have increased public awareness of the role of DNA testing in investigating crime. DNA clearly reveals whether someone is male or female. In a court of law, a man can be convicted of rape on the basis of DNA – no matter how he 'identifies'.

We are male or female by design.

## 1. Sexual Difference and Complementarity

Nature teaches us both the fundamental *distinction* and the necessary *complementarity* between men and women. As males or females, we have distinct and different capacity for reproduction. While appearance can be altered, this reproductive capacity cannot be adjusted.

When a man and a woman unite and a child is conceived, both parents have the same number of chromosomes. They are both equally human. But they are different: The woman with xx chromosones, and the man with xy chromosomes. There is also a complementary difference in the way the child is generated. The woman generates the child within her body, and the man generates the child in the woman's body.[1] If they conceive a little girl, then she develops in her mother's womb at the same time that her (the girl's) own egg cells are developing with her. A newborn baby girl has around two million eggs. When she becomes a woman, through her fertile life, around four hundred of her eggs will mature. When a boy reaches puberty, he can produce reproductive cells which mature into sperm cells.[2] 'Gender reassignment' is a parody of the real thing, and can never fulfil the creation design of fruitfulness.

Children and young people should be taught to respect the wonder of life, to respect their bodies, to respect the natural complementarity of the male and female body, and to respect their capacity to give birth to new life. When young people are taught the scientific facts about reproduction well, it should increase respect for sexual complementarity and it should inspire a greater respect and valuing of the opposite sex.[3] By contrast, the current trend to diminish the importance of sexual complementarity represents a profound disrespect for the human capacity to generate new life. Failure to respect sexual difference results in a disrespect for men and women. Popular culture celebrates androgyny – the blurring of gender roles. When gender activists get into classrooms, they

---

1    'The Fruitful Complementarity of Man and Woman: An Interview with Sister Mary Prudence Allen', National Catholic Register, 21 November, 2014, http://www.ncregister.com/daily-news/the-fruitful-complementarity-of-man-and-woman (accessed 24 November, 2018).

2    MacKellar, C, *The Image of God: Personhood and the Embryo*, SCM Press, p. 10.

3    Lovewise produces resources for children, young people, parents and teachers – resources which respect sexual complementarity and man-woman marriage. https://lovewise.org.uk/ (accessed 3 December 2018).

teach *anti-science* – telling children that 'not all boys have penises, and not all girls have vaginas'.

More than twenty years ago, before the transgender movement became mainstream, David Blankenhorn (founding president of the Institute for American Values) warned of the danger of blurring gender roles. He rightly observed that the 'infantile' desire to be both sexes at once is foolish and futile.

Indeed, androgyny [the combination of masculine and feminine characteristics into an ambiguous form] constitutes the most radical conception of expressive individualism that a society can imagine. It is the belief ... that human completion is a solo act. It is the insistence that the pathway to human happiness lies in transcending the old polarities of sexual embodiment for each individual man and woman to embrace and express all of human potentiality within his or her own self ... Like all forms of narcissism, its final product is not fulfilment but emptiness.[4]

More recently, the feminist academic and social critic Camille Paglia has poured scorn on the way that 'women's studies' programmes typically ignore biology.[5] The exclusion of any consideration of the basic biological differences between men and women, she suggests, lie behind the current denigration of motherhood, and the belittling of the male contribution to the building of civilisation.

The idea that we can 'change sex' is a parody of scientific reality. 'Every cell has a sex', so that men and women are profoundly

---

4    Blankenhorn, D, *Fatherless America: Confronting our most urgent social problem*, HarperPerenniel, 1995, pp. 122-3.

5    Paglia, C, *Free Women, Free Men*, Canongate Books, 2018, p. 216.

different in physiology and psychology. This has a significant impact on how they develop disease and how it should be treated.[6]

It also has a profound impact on areas such as sport. It has, until recently, been accepted that sport should be sex-segregated in the interest of fairness. In addition to the differences in chromosomes, hormone levels, primary and secondary sex characteristics, and reproductive capacity, there are numerous anatomical differences. Men are, on average, 10% taller than women; 15% heavier; and so on. There are numerous differences in body composition, significant cardiovascular differences and respiratory differences – all of which add up to significant performance advantages for men in most sports.[7]

Of course nature also teaches that there are sometimes problems in development. Babies may be born with any number of different abnormalities. But such conditions which result in a loss of biological functionality do not negate the norm.

## 2. God's Good Design

Christians affirm that God teaches us about His power and glory and beauty through nature, or the created order ('general revelation'). But to explain the significance of creation and the character of the Creator, God gives us 'special revelation' (His Word). There is harmony between these two sources of revelation.

The creation account shows us that binary is not bad; it is beautiful. When God separated light from darkness, land from sea, and earth from sky, He was bringing order out of chaos.

---

6    Paula Johnson, His and Hers Healthcare TED talk, https://www.youtube.com/watch?v=vhVWzkbAW4I (accessed 26 November 2018).

7    Ward, Keith, *Hands on Sports Therapy*, Cengage Learning, 2004.

After the flood, God promised that His good creation purpose would stand until the end of time. Note the binaries in this gracious covenant:

> While the earth remains,
> seed time and harvest,
> cold and heat,
> summer and winter,
> day and night
> shall not cease. (Gen. 8:22)

The first chapter of Genesis is punctuated with the repeated phrase 'God saw that it was good' (Gen. 1:10, 12, 18, 21, 25). Once man and woman had been created as the crowning achievement of God's creation, God saw that 'it was *very* good' (Gen. 1:31, emphasis mine). And the very first recorded spoken words of man are words of delight:

> 'This at last is bone of my bones and flesh of my flesh; she shall be called Woman, because she was taken out of Man.' (Gen. 2:23)

The creation account tells us that God created man and woman with equal dignity. Both were created to be made in 'the image' of God (Gen. 1:27). The invisible God would be represented on earth in visible, human form. Man and woman and their descendants would manage the earth, on His behalf, for His glory.

The fact that God created us in His image is the reason why every human life, male or female, from conception through to natural death, should be afforded dignity.

The creation account also makes it clear that God deliberately created man and woman with significant differences. Together, they had the capacity to be fruitful. Their bodily union had the potential to beget other humans, made in their image. By this means, the earth could be filled with people to carry out God's good purpose to manage and develop His creation. God created man and woman, and ordained man-woman marriage for all peoples at all times.

> So God created man in his own image, in the image of God he created him; male and female he created them. (Gen. 1:27)

> Therefore a man shall leave his father and his mother and hold fast to his wife, and they shall become one flesh. (Gen. 2:24)

This creation design is both assumed and affirmed by Jesus Christ:

> [Jesus] answered, 'Have you not read that he who created them from the beginning made them male and female, and said, "Therefore a man shall leave his father and his mother and hold fast to his wife, and the two shall become one flesh"? So they are no longer two but one flesh. What therefore God has joined together, let not man separate' (Matt. 19:4-6).

And also by the apostle Paul:

> Therefore a man shall leave his father and mother and hold fast to his wife, and the two shall become one flesh (Eph. 5:31).

## God's Good Design: Ruined, Redeemed, Restored

God's good design was wrecked by the entry of sin into the world. Genesis 3 describes the rebellion of our first parents against their Creator. The 'battle between the sexes' commenced at the Fall. Unhappiness, conflict, illness, and death: all these are the outworking of human sinfulness.[8] Where there is genuine gender

---

8   The outworking of human sinfulness occurs in a general sense: Jesus made it clear that there is not necessarily an automatically simplistic line to be

confusion, just as where there are any other serious psychological or physical problems, it is a tragic outworking of living in a world 'groaning' because of the effects of sin (Rom. 8:19-22); although, as Jesus made clear, it is *not* to be regarded as a result of an individual's specific sin (Luke 13:2).

Jesus Christ came into the world to reverse the effects of the Fall, and to restore God's creation. In this life we can begin to see the effects of the Fall being reversed. But we do not see that process completed until we are given perfect glorified resurrection bodies. The process of restoration will then be complete.

When Jesus Christ came into the world to reverse the effects of the Fall, He took human flesh, so that He could take on Himself the penalty for sin that humans had committed. Jesus Christ became a man, born of a woman. His physical body made visible what is invisible. As both perfect God and perfect man, Christ's work of redemption defeated sin, evil, Satan, and death itself. Jesus Christ is now raised (as a man) and lives and reigns as perfect God and perfect Man for all eternity. When we disparage the physical body, we disparage Christ. He lives and reigns forever, in His glorified resurrection body. His resurrection from the dead was the 'first fruits', guaranteeing the certain hope that believers can also look forward to being raised to life and being given perfect resurrection bodies (1 Cor. 15:12-58).

## God's Good Design: The Purpose Revealed

The New Testament explains that Christ's love for His people, His Bride, the Church, is the cosmic eternal reality (Eph. 5:25-32). God's creation of man and woman and His design for man-woman marriage is a signpost pointing to that greater reality.

---

drawn connecting an individual's illness with personal sin (John 9:3).

The Bible begins with a marriage: the coming together of male and female. The two became one flesh. Marital union signifies the close and loving union between Christ and the Church. The Bible ends as it began, with a marriage: the marriage supper of the Lamb. The coming together of Christ and the Church is the moment to which earthly marriage points. The fellowship and union of Christ and His people endures through eternity, long after the temporal earthly signpost of human marriage has come to an end.

To disparage the physical human body is to disparage the God in whose image we are made. To downplay the male-female distinction is to reject God's design.

## 3. The Good Design Demeaned

Gender ideology downplays the significance of our physical bodies, and says that our subjective feelings are more important. It places a wedge between body and mind. This false distinction between body and mind is a new form of an old heresy called Gnosticism.[9] It divides your thoughts from the physical reality of the body. It says that your mind, your soul, your thoughts, are more important, and can overrule the physical facts. In New Testament times, this heresy claimed that Jesus may have risen from the dead spiritually, but not physically.

How does this play out in real life? In 2018, a father of seven, who was also a violent and dangerous criminal, said that he believed he was a woman. An appeal judge in the UK said that on that basis, he could be recognised as female and placed in a female prison. It didn't matter that biologically and physically this person

---

9    Gnosticism, The Christian Institute, https://www.christian.org.uk/wp-content/uploads/gnosticism.pdf

was male.[10] If in his mind he 'thought' he was female, that was what counted. But he used his male body to abuse female prisoners. So much for the 'irrelevance' of the body.[11]

This shocking failure to protect female prisoners was discussed by British Members of Parliament when (in November 2018) they debated the issue of 'self-declaration' – that is, whether people should be allowed to transition without any medical referral. The following exchange between Mr David TC Davis and Ms Layla Moran revealed that Ms Moran is a modern-day Gnostic. David Davis believes that a person with a penis cannot be a woman. Layla Moran believes that a person with a penis *is* a woman *if he claims to be one*. Mr Davis asked Ms Moran whether she would be happy sharing a changing room with someone with a male body who claimed to be female. She replied:

There are many forms of the human body. **I see someone in their soul** and as a person. I do not really care whether they have a male body.[12]

---

10 'Trans criminal father of 7 can swap gender despite doctor's doubts', *Daily Mail*, 17 October, 2018, https://www.pressreader.com/uk/daily-mail/20181017/282067687903847 (accessed 16 November, 2018).

11 A three-year study of transsexuals at Charing Cross Hospital Gender Identity Clinic in the 1980s found that over half of the male-to-female patients and about one third of the female-to-male patients had criminal backgrounds. Tully, Brian, Accounting for Transsexualism, London, 1992, p. 267; quoted in Carys Moseley, 'The Rise and Normalisation of Transgenderism', Affinity Social Issues Bulletin, February 2019. Today in the UK however, police forces do not record the transgender status and biological sex of people charged with crimes, which limits discussion of transgenderism and crime.

12 House of Commons, Hansard, Debate on Self-Identification of Gender, 21 November 2018, https://hansard.parliament.uk/commons/2018-11-21/debates/BE06C5D4-E549-4F94-87B1-9B77F32EA155/Self-IdentificationOfGender (accessed 26 November 2018).

Layla Moran claims to be able to see someone's 'soul'. Most of us don't claim to be able to do that! And she is driving a false wedge between body and soul.

If the new Gnostics win the battle of ideas, people with female bodies will lose the right to separate themselves in any context from people with male bodies. The new Gnostics will abolish the right to protect the privacy of our daughters and granddaughters (and sons and grandsons).

Gnosticism divides what God has united. He made us whole people. Our body, our mind, and our spirit or soul are not to be divided or played off against each other. God specifically designs and determines our body. It reflects His intent. It is not irrelevant (Ps. 139:13-14; Jer. 1:5). God deliberately created male and female as different and interdependent beings (Gen. 2:18; 21-24), and He prohibits the blurring of gender identity (Deut. 22:5).

It is common today to make a false distinction between biological life (the physical body) and 'personhood'. This false distinction is used to justify abortion (the embryo is clearly human, but is denied 'personhood' as it can't yet communicate/relate, etc). This false distinction can be used to justify killing people who have 'lost capacity' due to accident, illness, or old age (the argument is that they are no longer 'persons' if they can't communicate, etc.) Those with 'personhood' are protected, but 'bodies' have no inherent rights or dignity. They can be killed, used for 'spare parts', or experimented on. Nancy Pearcey observes:

> The body is denigrated to the level of the sub-personal. It is trivialized as a form of raw material that can be tinkered with, manipulated, experimented on, or destroyed with no moral significance. Human life is reduced to a utilitarian calculus, subject only to a cost-benefit

analysis. This is a far lower view of human life than anything taught in biblical Christianity.[13]

## Escape from Reason

To defy nature and deny our creation design means we defy reason. We embrace unreason and insanity.

Fifty years ago, the great Christian thinker Francis Schaeffer wrote *Escape from Reason*. He warned that we are witnessing the denial of reality. He pointed to the French philosopher and social theorist Michel Foucault, and his book, *Madness and Civilisation*. Foucault carried Rousseau's thinking to its logical conclusion:

> The ultimate in autonomous freedom is being crazy. It's a fine thing to be crazy, for then you are free.[14]

Fast forward to 2018, to a school in Brighton, England where trans-affirming organisations have been particularly active. 40 children in that one school have identified as 'trans' and 36 as 'gender fluid'.[15] Those who say they are 'gender fluid' want to be free to change identity from day to day. That is a denial of reality. That kind of 'freedom' is no freedom at all. To pander to it is not kindness. It is to play along with unreason and insanity.

---

13  Pearcey, N, *Saving Leonardo*, B & H Publishing, 2010.

14  Schaeffer, F, *Escape from Reason*, Intervarsity Press, 1968, p. 70.

15  Danyal Hussain, 'Fashionable Brighton school has 40 children who do not identify with their sex and birth and another 36 are 'gender fluid', *Daily Mail*, 26 November, 2018, https://www.dailymail.co.uk/news/article-6426961/Fashionable-Brighton-school-40-children-not-identify-sex-birth.html (accessed 26 November 2018).

## 4. Rejection of the Good Design

After the creation of man and woman, God declared that His creation was 'very good'.

But rejecting the idea of our Creator God means that we reject His creation as a 'given' to be respected – and that we demand the right to de-construct and re-construct it as we please, to suit ourselves.

In Spring 2018, the leading fashion house, Gucci, put on their celebrated show. Already celebrated for provocative transgressiveness (for example, showing male and female fashion on both genders), this time the set was designed in the style of an operating theatre. Two of the models paraded down the runway carrying exact models of their own severed heads, instead of handbags. Another walked down with a 'third eye' (an exact copy of her own two) fixed on her forehead. A tweet from Gucci explained:

> The concept of the operating room reflects the work of a designer –
> the act of cutting, splicing, and reconstructing materials and fabrics
> to create a new personality and identity with them. [16]

But here, the designer didn't draw the line at cutting and splicing clothing – he went onto depict the cutting and splicing of the human body itself. So another Gucci tweet commented:

> The hybrid is metaphorically praised as a figure that can overcome
> the dualism and dichotomy of identity.[17]

---

16  https://www.glamour.com/story/gucci-faux-severed-heads-fall-2018-runway (accessed 6 December 2018).

17  Ibid.

The sheer ugliness of the spectacle was a tragic reflection on a worldview that says we have the right to deconstruct and reconstruct our own bodies.

It is this worldview that has led to an epidemic of young girls seeking to 'bind' their developing breasts in a vain effort to deny their blossoming womanhood. Even worse, some young girls demand the surgical removal of perfectly healthy breasts. It is the world-view that leads to young men trying to 'tuck' (conceal) their genitals and demanding female hormones in an effort to suppress their manhood. Tragically, some young men demand surgical removal of their genitalia: a non-reversible mutilation of a healthy body.

All this is just a symptom of this generation's declaration of independence from our Creator God. The demand for absolute personal freedom means that we do not have to answer to God or to anyone else. It means that we must be free to choose our own identity and make our own rules. As the atheist philosopher Friedrich Nietzsche said, 'If God is dead, then all things are possible.'

If there is no God, and we are the only point of reference, then how do we know what, or who, we are? We cannot know who we are unless we know who God is.[18] The Christian worldview begins with Creation. Our triune, personal, relational God created men and women in His own image – to relate to Him, and to relate to each other.

## Expressive Individualism

Once we deny that there is a God whose character and decree defines what is right, then we deny that there are moral laws that are

---

18    Calvin, John, *Institutes of the Christian Religion*, ed. McNeill, J, trans. Battles, F. L, Westminster Press, Vol. 1, Chapter 1, p. 37.

true for everyone, at every time, in every place. The only remaining moral absolute is to be faithful to yourself, or to find your own identity. This can be described as 'expressive individualism'. By contrast, the Bible teaches that all humans have the knowledge of God's moral law in their hearts, and we will each be judged according to the conscience He has given us.

The end point of expressive individualism is absolute independence – and the expectation that, on my own, I can 'be' all I need. But any form of 'need' or interdependence is seen as weakness in a fiercely individualistic age. People demand the 'human right' to reproduce, by themselves, (with the goal of raising the child without a father). Their demand to be recognised as 'non-binary' is consistent with rejection of God's design for complementarity. It reflects the proud desire of each individual to be self-sufficient, effectively to be both man and woman. But it defies the creation order. It is symptomatic of rebellion against God's design for complementarity between the sexes, which ensures that in family and in community we 'need' each other.

## A False Gospel

The entry of sin into the world left humans alienated from our Creator and alienated from one another. The good news of the Gospel tells us that rescue from that alienation is offered to all who will repent of sin, receive God's offer of forgiveness, and submit to Jesus Christ as Lord. In order to repent, we need to feel a deep sorrow for sin, and a determination to turn away from it.

But in our day, calls for repentance have been defined as abuse, and submission is regarded as repressive.

On the one hand, if someone feels 'shame' in their identity, they should hear the biblical and liberating truth that (in reality) 'identity' is not a 'feeling' about 'gender'. Our identity as a human is that of having been made in the image of God – and every person is therefore of infinite worth. But, equally, a sense of guilt and 'shame' at sin is what drives us to seek forgiveness. Conviction of sin is the work of the Holy Spirit. Today, even in evangelical circles, it is often unpopular to speak of conviction, sin, and repentance.

So, in place of the biblical Gospel, we have a new salvation message: You can be whoever you want to be! You can do what you want! You can define yourself as you like! You don't have to feel guilty about anything and you don't have to fear judgment!

This is a false gospel. It is another re-run of Genesis 3. It challenges the truth of God's Word: 'Did God actually say, "You shall not?"' (Gen. 3:1) and offers a false reward for disobedience: 'You will be like God' (Gen. 3:5). It is the old rebellion in new clothes. It is the human desire to be master; to recognise no God but me. And this false gospel is even being proclaimed in some sections of the Church.

## 5. Compromise in the Church: The Culture of Limitless Self-Regard

One would expect that the Christian Church would unite in speaking out *for* God's creation design, and *against* gender theory.

But many sections of the church have bought into the current world-view of 'expressive individualism'. Individual human experience is often placed 'over' Scripture. If the Bible contradicts what 'I sincerely and deeply feel', then my 'sincere and deep feelings' win. This is simply the current outworking of theological liberalism. Theological liberals in the nineteenth and twentieth centuries placed human *reason* above Scripture. In the twenty-first century, their descendants place human *experience* above Scripture. Emotion and sentiment win. Many in the professing church have gone along with the current idolisation of erotic and romantic love. So, for example, teaching on marital fidelity has been diluted – to allow for 'individual fulfilment'.

For some Christian leaders, the worst crime is to make people feel guilt or shame. Such people have absorbed the thinking of psychologists such as Freud. Many theologically liberal churches embrace the demands of LGBT campaigners (and current equality legislation and diversity training). The assumption behind all this is that it is abusive to make anyone feel shame or guilt. Only two options are possible: celebration of LGBT identities (the 'moral' option), or homophobic rejection (the 'immoral' option). Celebration of LGBT identities is described by some as the 'truly Christian' ethic. Why?

The British Anglican clergyman, Rev Dr Gavin Ashenden, helpfully explains that 'hate' has been redefined to include 'any criticism of the fragile self'.[19] He recalls his ministerial training, where he was taught the two core elements of Rogerian counselling technique: *unconditional positive regard* and *self-actualisation*. This means, in practice, that people commonly think of 'love' as being uncritical affirmation. We are told to accept someone as they are.[20] 'Hate' has been redefined. It is now defined as being any questioning or criticism of the demanding ego:

> If, in the name of an external morality, a Christian voice were to challenge the demands the therapised ego insisted made it happy or actualised, this Christian voice/call, or the Bible whose words the Christian was calling upon, would become 'hate speech' .... The culture of Limitless Self-Regard ... identifies any refusal to accept

---

19  Ashenden, G, 'Redefining hate: from diabolical anti-love to any criticism of the fragile self', Guest post on Archbishop Cranmer website, 14 July 2017, see http://archbishopcranmer.com/redefining-hate-diabolical-anti-love-criticism-self/ (accessed 21 September 2017).

20  Ibid, p. 4.

its demands for self-realisation or self-satisfaction on its own terms as hate. The struggle in the Church is not one of compassion versus hate: it is one of revelation versus narcissism.[21]

In this current therapeutic culture, to challenge any individual's claim to their own unique 'identity' or 'orientation' is viewed as being hateful. That is why Swedish Pentecostal pastor Ake Green, who preached a sermon on the immorality of homosexual behaviour, was prosecuted in 2005 and was sentenced to a month in prison for the crime of hate speech (he appealed the sentence, and it was later overturned).[22]

We must not be intimidated. What is the logical outcome of such thinking? Do we have to affirm every 'identity' or 'orientation'? What about paedophilia? Or bestiality? Or what about those who claim to be a different age? Or race? Or species? The culture of 'limitless self-regard' has no end point.

## 6. The need to stand firm

The New Testament warns us that there will be those in the professing church who embrace falsehood and heresy. Current Western culture places each person's individual desires as the source of authority for them. Each person is told they can define themselves, and live as they choose. But we are to stand firm on the foundation of God's revealed will, so clearly expressed in both general and special revelation. We are not to be alarmed or fearful. We are to be confident in the unchanging truth of God's Word, which shines out as a light in the darkest of times.

---

21  Ibid, pp. 5-7.

22  Vanderheyden, T, 'Swedish Pastor Ake Green Acquitted of Hate Speech against Homosexuals', Life Site News, 29 November 2005, https://www.lifesitenews.com/news/swedish-pastor-ake-green-acquitted-of-hate-speech-against-homosexuals (accessed 5 December 2018).

We need to distinguish between people who are caught up in this confusion and are suffering greatly, from activists who are lobbying for transgender rights.[23] Those who are suffering must be treated with respect and compassion. Christians often stop there, and fail to challenge the false teaching that is causing confusion. We must not be naive. Activists for trans rights are not just wanting toleration for a small minority of troubled people. They want to enforce a false ideology on everyone else. They want to change the way we speak, and change the way we and our children think. This is a unique form of intolerance. We are told to address men as if they are women, women as men, or people who demand it as 'non-binary'. A new faith is being imposed by force.

Our creation design teaches us that God has made us male and female to reflect His glory in every age. This foundational creation reality is transcultural and atemporal. Scripture does not, cannot, and will not allow the false split between sex and so-called 'gender'. The demand for a genderless body is to unravel the creation design and go back to chaos.

The theory that binary is bad and that we can construct our own gendered identity is an attack on humanity's having been made in the image of God, male and female. Attacking humankind made in the image of God is an attack on God Himself, and is an assault on the authority of His Word. That is why this is a conscience issue for many Christians. We should not push Christians to go against their God-given conscience. We must learn from history that Christians in every age may face pressure to speak words that are untrue. Some give in, but others are willing to die rather than speak untruth.

---

23    Bannerman, L, 'Trans movement has been hijacked by bullies and trolls', *The Times*, 1 October 2018, https://www.thetimes.co.uk/article/trans-movement-has-been-hijacked-by-bullies-and-trolls-lwl3s73vj (accessed 3 December 2018).

In the early church, there was the demand that the early Christians say the words 'Caesar is Lord'. Of course they were also allowed to say 'Jesus is Lord' (alongside Caesar). Many could and did rationalise the compromise. Many others were willing to die rather than compromise.

We need to stand firm. We can stand in unity with all those of different faiths, or none, who see from nature that boys cannot be girls, and men cannot be women. We can stand in unity with those who demand freedom to speak the truth and refuse to be bullied into going along with such nonsense. This can include people like Jordan Peterson, Professor of Psychology at Toronto University. He believes that when it comes to being told to tell lies, there are only two choices:

> There are only two alternatives. One is silent slavery – with all the repression and resentment that will generate. The other is outright conflict. Free speech is not just another value. It's the foundation of Western Civilisation.[24]

Likewise, Douglas Murray (who himself is atheist and gay) comments that people now are being instructed to tell the lie that:

> There is no difference between men and women and that we can migrate between the sexes and that our bodies are like pieces of Lego – you can just stick bits on to it and if you don't like it you can take it off again.

But he warns:

---

there is something demoralizing about agreeing to lie.... Truth is energising.[25]

## Further Reading

Nancy Pearcey, *Love Thy Body: Answering Hard Questions about Life and Sexuality*, Baker, 2018.

---

25   Van Maren, Jonathan, 'Prominent Gay Atheist: Transgenderism is a "lie": Agreeing to it demoralizes you', *LifeSite*, 30 May, 2019, https://www.lifesitenews.com/blogs/prominent-gay-atheist-transgenderism-is-a-lie (accessed 6 June, 2019).

# 6.
# The 'Transgendering' of Children

Little Poppy went to school,
There she learned that trans is cool.[1]

C hildren learn through storytelling. Each culture has its favourite children's tales. One of the most popular, with variants across many cultures, is 'Cinderella'. This well-loved story has now been retold for little ones with a sinister twist. In *Jamie: A Transgender Cinderella Story*, Jamie is a girl. She's great at fixing things. So she realises that she must be a boy! Jamie manages to get to the ball (dressed as a boy, with a great new haircut). She dances with the princess. They fall in love and leave the ball in the pumpkin car Jamie has been clever enough to make.[2] And they live happily ever after.

---

1     Adapted from Brown, M. L, *A Queer Thing Happened to America: And what a long, strange trip it's been,* EqualTime Books, 2011, pp. 86-7.

2     Pike, O, *Jamie: A Transgender Cinderella Story* (Oliver Pike, 2015), https://www.youtube.com/watch?v=4_9F0RZUsIc (accessed 13 November, 2016).

Such ideas only sow seeds of confusion. Our children are being robbed of truth. They are being cheated of the security that comes from clear boundaries. And at an ever younger age, they are expected to construct their own identities.

In this chapter, first we will distinguish two different types of gender dysphoria: *child-onset gender dysphoria* and *rapid-onset dysphoria* which occurs mostly among adolescents. In each case, we consider the debate around 'treatments'. Next, we discuss some of the cultural influences leading to gender confusion among children and young people. We will then examine the pressure to promote gender theory to children through schools. Most worrying of all, we see that children are being used as pawns by gender activists. Finally, we consider how parents might respond.

## 1. Childhood-onset dysphoria

Remember Ryland? This little girl began saying that she wanted to be a boy as soon as she could talk (see the Introduction). Some children, both boys and girls, exhibit 'gender-nonconforming behaviour' from an early age. Gender nonconformity may express itself in strong preferences to behave like the other sex with regard to clothing, play styles, playmates, interests, and so on. A gender-nonconforming boy will often be ostracised or bullied by others who shame him with terms such as 'sissy'. A gender-nonconforming girl may be teased as a 'tomboy'. Such children are unhappy with their birth sex. They may long to be the other sex. They may even assert that they 'are' the other sex, they may claim they have been 'given the wrong body'.

Children with autistic traits seem, for complex reasons, sometimes likely to experience a measure of gender nonconformity.[3]

---

3    Ehrhard, Elise, 'The Transgender Movement targets Autistic Children', *Crisis Magazine*, 12 December, 2016, https://www.crisismagazine.

In recent years, activists have sometimes pushed such children or young people towards the idea that gender transition may help them. In reality, as one parent argues cogently,

> Encouraging sex-change or an alternate gender identity is destructive to individuals with autism or Asperger's (previously in a separate diagnostic category), only furthering their private pain.[4]

When gender-nonconforming children are *not* encouraged to identify as the opposite sex the great majority (between 60 and 90%) adjust to their birth sex, once puberty has occurred. Compared with other children, gender-nonconforming boys are more likely in later life to experience same-sex attraction; this outcome is less likely among girls.[5] Of course, all bullying is unacceptable in any context. Such children should be protected from bullying as much as possible.

A comprehensive overview of research on gender identity issues concluded:

> In the course of their development, many children explore the idea of being of the opposite sex ... nearly all children ultimately identify with their biological sex. The notion that a two-year-old, having expressed thoughts or behaviours identified with the opposite sex, can be labelled for life as transgender has absolutely no support in science. Indeed, it is iniquitous to believe that all children who have gender-atypical thoughts or behaviour at some point in their

---

com/2016/autism-transgendered-movement (accessed 24 May, 2019).

4 Ibid.

5 Bailey, J. M, and Blanchard, R, 'Gender Dysphoria is not one thing', *4thWaveNow*, 7 December, 2017, https://4thwavenow.com/2017/12/07/gender-dysphoria-is-not-one-thing/ (accessed 23 May, 2019).

development, particularly before puberty, should be encouraged to become transgender.[6]

There is vigorous debate about what is the appropriate treatment for children who are conflicted about their gender. In the past, 'watchful waiting' was advised by professionals. That is because if social transition is permitted, the dysphoria will almost certainly persist.[7] If social transition is *not* permitted, most children 'desist' once puberty has occurred.[8]

In response to pressure from activists, there is an increasing tendency to insist that children demonstrating gender nonconformity should be allowed, if they wish, to 'socially transition'. 'Social transition' means adopting the name, pronouns, clothes, hairstyle, etc., of the opposite sex, and allowing the child to use the toilet and other facilities of the other sex.

Parents, and others, who resist this are sometimes accused of 'transphobia'. But they are right to resist! That is because there's a totally natural way of resolving childhood gender confusion. It's called puberty. When children do genuinely experience discontent with their biological sex, this resolves itself in up to 90% of cases if puberty is allowed to take its course. If you allow testosterone

---

6    Mayer L. S, and McHugh, P. R, eds., 'Sexuality and Gender: Findings from the Biological, Psychological, and Social Sciences', *The New Atlantis*, Special Report, No 50, Fall 2016, p.6.

7    Bailey, J. M, and Blanchard, R, 'Gender Dysphoria is not one thing'.

8    'Watchful waiting' was advocated by Dr Kenneth J. Zucker, a world-leading clinician, who followed the principle that congruence between a patient's felt gender identity and birth sex is the best outcome. He was wrongly dismissed and defamed, due to activist pressure, but won a public apology in 2018. Kearns, Madeleine, 'Dr Zucker Defied Trans Orthodoxy. Now he's vindicated', *NRPlus*, 25 October, 2018, https://www.nationalreview.com/2018/10/transgender-orthodoxy-kenneth-zucker-vindicated/ (accessed 24 May, 2019).

to kick in for boys, and oestrogen for girls, in the vast majority of cases gender confusion is resolved.

Dr Michael Bailey and Dr Ray Blanchard advise parents of children below puberty to:

Firmly (but kindly and patiently) insist that your child is a member of his/her birth sex. You should not allow your child to engage in behaviours such as cross dressing and fantasy play as the other sex. Above all else, you should not let your child socially transition to the other sex.[9]

Glen Stanton writes:

The push in culture today to embrace and affirm such children's wishes is founded more upon a political ideology than it is in careful science and experience.[10]

Sadly, this 'political ideology' has led in some countries to an increased expectation that children demonstrating gender nonconformity should be prescribed with puberty suppression drugs (hypothalamic hormone suppression at ages 10-13) as a means of making 'sex reassignment' less traumatic in later adolescence. These drugs were first used to block puberty in the Netherlands in 2001. There have been no long-term clinical trials. Children may demand that their parents allow them to request such drugs. The argument is that if gender dysphoria persists, and they pursue the course of 'sex reassignment,'[11] it will be less

---

9    Bailey, J. M, and Blanchard, R, 'Gender Dysphoria is not one thing'.

10    Stanton, G, 'Boys, Girls, Other: Making Sense of the Confusing New World of Gender Identity', Family First New Zealand, 2015, page 6, see http://askmefirst.nz/wp-content/uploads/2016/08/Boys-Girls-Other-FULL-REPORT.pdf

11    'Sex reassignment' is increasingly referred to as 'gender confirmation', in keeping with the idea that each person has a 'gender identity' which may be

traumatic if normal physical development has been suppressed. It is claimed that the effects of such drugs are 'fully reversible'. But there is no long-term evidence to prove this claim. A study conducted at the Tavistock Clinic in London found that no patient taking puberty blockers later desisted – whereas 90.3% of children who did not take them did later desist.[12] The publication of this study was blocked.[13]

'Treatment' has rushed ahead of research. Children and young people are moving down the track of life-changing procedures. Future fertility is threatened. And all of this is being pushed without proper medical diagnoses. There is no long-term evidence to prove that puberty blockers are safe. Rather, there is some evidence that they can result in decreased bone mineralisation (meaning a higher risk of fractures), and an increased risk of obesity and testicular cancer in boys. Oxford University's Centre of Evidence-Based Medicine recently reviewed research into the drugs. Professor Carl Heneghan concluded that blocking puberty was an 'unregulated live experiment on children'.[14] There is strong evidence that the drugs negatively impact bone development, and

---

at varience with their biological sex.

12  World Professional Association for Transgender Health, WPATH, Symposium 17-21 June 2016, 'Gender Dysphoria in Younger Children: Support and Care in an Evolving Environment', Dr Polly Carmichael et al., http://wpath2016.conferencespot.org/62620-wpathv2-1.3138789/t001-1.3140111/f009a-1.3140266/0706-000523-1.3140268 (accessed 24 May, 2019).

13  Biggs, M, 'Tavistock's Experimentation with Puberty Blockers: Scrutinizing the Evidence', *Transgender Trend*, 2 March, 2019, https://www.transgendertrend.com/tavistock-experiment-puberty-blockers/ (accessed 24 May, 2019).

14  Bannerman, Lucy, 'Calls to end transgender "experiment on children"', *The Times*, 8 April, 2019, https://www.thetimes.co.uk/article/calls-to-end-transgender-experiment-on-children-k792rfj7d (accessed 29 May, 2019).

may also effect height, organ development, and bodily shape.[15] The *British Medical Journal* published a letter in January 2019 by three doctors who argued that the use of puberty blocking medication:

> leaves a young person in developmental limbo without the benefit of pubertal hormones or secondary sex characteristics, which would tend to consolidate gender identity ... [and] is likely to threaten the maturation of the adolescent mind ... to halt the natural process of puberty is an intervention of momentous proportions with lifelong medical, psychological and emotional implications.[16]

## 2. Rapid-onset dysphoria

In recent years, a growing number of adolescents who have not previously demonstrated gender nonconformity have been experiencing 'rapid-onset gender dysphoria' (ROGD). This seems mostly, but not always, to occur among girls. This sometimes seems to come from nowhere, and parents are bewildered. The first major study of this was conducted by Lisa Littman, and her findings were published in 2018.[17] There was intense controversy, and she was challenged, but in March 2019 the study was republished, with the methods and findings having remained mostly unchanged.

Littman found that adolescents experiencing ROGD tended to either belong to a group of friends in which multiple, or even all,

---

15  Hruz, Paul W, Mayer, Lawrence, McHugh, Paul R, 'Growing Pains: Problems with Puberty Suppression in Treating Gender Dysphoria, *The New Atlantis*, 2017, https://www.thenewatlantis.com/publications/growing-pains (accessed 29 May, 2019).

16  Richard, C, Maxell, J, McCune, N, *British Medical Journal*, 17 January, 2019.

17  Littman, Lisa, 'Rapid-Onset Gender Dysphoria in Adolescents and Young Adults: A Study of Parental Reports', PLOS ONE, 2018, https://journals.plos.org/plosone/article?id=10.1371/journal.pone.0202330 (accessed 24 May, 2019).

members became transgender-identified around the same time, or that they were immersed in social media, or both. She described this as 'social contagion'. A peer group (either real or virtual) fosters the mutual belief that anxiety and unhappiness may be caused by being 'transgender', and that 'gender transition' will provide the solution. Even a cursory trawl through social media sites such as Tumblr reveals an array of heart-breaking posts evidencing deep self-hatred, coupled with a naive confidence that 'transition' will lead to acceptance by peers and internal peace. And one can see the angst and agony of such youngsters shamelessly being exploited by the commercial promotion of products such as breast binders.

Young people learn what to demand and what to say from others, especially online. They are told by trans-affirming peers that parents who resist such demands are 'transphobic'. They are warned that Christians who believe that God created male and female are 'bigoted'. There is a sense that the world is divided: 'us' (those who understand trans issues) and 'them' (the enemy). There is encouragement to cut ties with biological family members and others who don't endorse the demand to transition. They are told that young people who aren't allowed to transition are 'likely to commit suicide'; and misleading suicide statistics are spread around.[18] Worried parents may be terrified into acquiescence, and say: 'I want a happy daughter, not a dead son'.[19]

---

18  'A Scientist Reviews Transgender Suicide Stats', Transgender Trend, 3 December 2016, see https://www.transgendertrend.com/a-scientist-reviews-transgender-suicide-stats/ (accessed 12 May 2017). This article challenges the statistics used by Mermaids, a lobby group which encourages children to be free to change sex, and threatens parents who resist the prospect of their child committing suicide.

19  *Transgender Children and Young People*, Cambridge Scholars Press, 2016, pp. 17-18.

There is mutual pressure to move down the route of demanding hormonal treatments. Increasing numbers of girls are 'binding' their breasts when they start developing, and boys may seek to conceal (tuck) their genitals. At around the age of 16, 'cross-sex' hormones may be given. Girls may be able to have a double mastectomy (the removal of breasts). Some youngsters also demand so-called 'bottom surgeries' or genital reassignment surgeries, although these are not recommended before age 18.

But, equally, there are many testimonies on social media sites which reveal the heartbreak of those who later desist, and who testify to the lasting physical and emotional harm of these measures. For example, girls find that breast binding decreases lung capacity and can lead to breathing difficulties, fainting, broken ribs, and back pain. If the youngster does take cross-sex hormones, the risks include cardiac disease, high blood pressure, blood clots, strokes, diabetes, and cancers.[20] Surgeries, of course, are irreversible; and they are often regretted. Risky and dangerous 'treatments' are handed out to gender-confused youngsters. Such treatments do not guarantee any resolution of their confusion, and result in lasting damage.

Dr Michael Bailey and Dr Ray Blanchard believe that:

ROGD is not about discovering gender dysphoria that was there all along; rather, it is about falsely coming to believe that one's problems have been due to gender dysphoria previously hidden (from the self and others) ... People with ROGD do have a kind of gender dysphoria, but it is gender dysphoria due to persuasion of those

---

20    Cretella, M, 'I'm a Pediatrician: How Transgender Ideology has Infiltrated My Field and Produced Large-Scale Sex Abuse', *The Daily Signal*, 3 July 2017, https://www.dailysignal.com/2017/07/03/im-pediatrician-transgender-ideology-infiltrated-field-produced-large-scale-child-abuse/ (accessed 5 December, 2018).

especially vulnerable to a false idea. It is not gender dysphoria due to anything like having the mind/brain of one sex trapped in the body of the other.[21]

And, condemning the 'treatments' handed out to both children with early onset dysphoria and adolescents with rapid onset dysphoria, American pediatrician, Dr Michelle Cretella argues:

> These professionals are using the myth that people are born transgender to justify engaging in massive, uncontrolled, and unconsented experimentation on children who have a psychological condition that would otherwise resolve after puberty in the vast majority of cases. Today's institutions that promote transition affirmation are pushing children to impersonate the opposite sex, sending many of them down the path of puberty blockers, sterilization, the removal of healthy body parts, and untold psychological damage. These harms constitute nothing less than institutionalized child abuse. Sound ethics demand an immediate end to the use of pubertal suppression, cross-sex hormones, and sex reassignment surgeries in children and adolescents, as well as an end to promoting gender ideology via school curricula and legislative policies.[22]

## 3. Why so much confusion?

Children and young people are not only receiving confusing messages from school. For a whole variety of reasons, increasing numbers of young people are confused and unhappy about their bodies and their identity.

---

21  Bailey, J. M, and Blanchard, R, 'Gender Dysphoria is not one thing'.

22  Cretella, M, 'I'm a Pediatrician: How Transgender Ideology has Infiltrated My Field and Produced Large-Scale Sex Abuse'.

## The sexualisation of culture

The radical feminist movement campaigned for women to 'enjoy' the same sexual freedoms as men. This contributed to the sexualisation of Western culture. Pornography is ubiquitous, and it is being accessed by an ever-younger demographic. But pornography only fuels the sexual harassment of girls: 'Sexual harassment and assault of girls in schools has reached epidemic proportions.'[23] Girls are being relentlessly judged by appearance. If they don't relish the prospect of being sexually available to men from an unnaturally early age, they are mocked as being prudish virgins. If they don't want to engage in hours of expensive beauty maintenance and starve themselves into being unnaturally thin, they may be dismissed as ugly, or even be labelled as being lesbian. All of these pressures contribute to

> lack of confidence in, and comfort with, own body, disassociation, shame, anxiety, self-disgust, low self-esteem, depression, negative mood, eating disorders, negative body image and sense of self, self-objectification and self-harming behaviours.[24]

Some may conclude that if being a 'successful girl' must mean looking and behaving like a porn star, they'd rather not be girls at all. Girls who have been victims of sexual abuse may find it safer to identify as a boy.[25]

In our over-sexualised culture, there is almost as much pressure on young men to present an idealised male body. If a boy is smaller

---

23  Davies-Arai, S, 'The Transgender Experiment on Children', in *Transgender Children and Young People*, Cambridge Scholars Press, 2016, p. 29.

24  Ibid, p. 28.

25  'Attachment Patterns and Complex Trauma in a Sample of Adults Diagnosed with Gender Dysphoria', https://www.ncbi.nlm.nih.gov/pmc/articles/PMC5799708/ (accessed 3 August 2019).

than average, bad at sports, and judged to be effeminate, he may be bullied. If a boy has negative male role models in his own life, or if he has been exposed to violent pornography, or been sexually abused by a male, he may associate masculinity with violence, and decide that he doesn't want to be male at all.[26]

## Family Breakdown – fewer stable role models

Rates of fatherlessness in the twenty-first century are probably unprecedented. Globally, illegitimacy rates are rising dramatically. In 1964, only four small countries (Austria, Latvia, Iceland and Sweden) had more than ten per cent of children born outside marriage. By 2016, more than 60 per cent of children were born outside marriage in twenty-five countries. A further twenty countries – including Belgium, Denmark, Norway, France and Sweden – all had more than fifty per cent of children born outside marriage.[27]

This all means that fewer children experience the unbroken stability of their own two natural parents staying together throughout their developing years. Fewer children have stable role models of a mother and a father. Fewer are able to experience positive role models of healthy masculinity and femininity.

## Construct your own (special) identity!

When increasing numbers of children are suffering emotional and mental distress, unhappiness and confusion is only compounded

---

26  'Sexual Violence History and Welfare in Transgender People', https://journals.sagepub.com/doi/abs/10.1177/0886260516657911, (accessed 3 August 2019); David Bell, 'Report on Gender Identity Development Service at Tavistock Clinic', not made public to date, but see https://www.thetimes.co.uk/article/staff-at-trans-clinic-fear-damage-to-children-as-activists-pile-on-pressure-c5k655nq9, (accessed 3 August, 2019).

27  Chamie, J, 'Out-of-wedlock births rise Wordwide', Yale Global Online, 16 March 2017, https://yaleglobal.yale.edu/content/out-wedlock-births-rise-worldwide (accessed 14 August 2018).

when they are taught that they must construct their own identity. Children don't thrive when they're not allowed to simply be confident in their own bodies – confident that they are a boy or a girl. They need boundaries, not for everything to be fluid and uncertain. But in the Instagram age, young people are constantly having to present themselves to others in an original way. Each one has to appear 'special' and unique. Then zealous campaigners for 'diversity' lay out a smorgasbord of gender options from which they must take their pick. Those who see others celebrated for being different are attracted to the possibility of being different, too. To be boring, conformist, and unnoticed – in a culture of expressive individualism – is not good news.

Children are getting the message from social media, films, TV, and from their friends that some people are 'born in the wrong body'. (There is absolutely no scientific evidence for this, as 'twin' studies have shown).[28] Unhappy and confused children (including those suffering from abuse) are promised that if they 'change gender', their problems may be resolved. British journalist Andrew Gilligan writes:

> In thousands of Instagram posts, Tumblr messages and YouTube 'vlogs', impressionable young people, largely girls, are told by upbeat, pretty folk slightly older than themselves how transitioning can be an escape route from uncertainty, autism, friendlessness, abuse, the pains of puberty, or homosexuality.[29]

---

28  Mayer, L. S and McHugh, P. R, eds., 'Sexuality and Gender: Findings from the Biological, Psychological, and Social Sciences', pp. 98-9; Cretella, M, 'I'm a Pediatrician. How Transgender Ideology has Infiltrated my Field and Produced Large-Scale Child Abuse', gives evidence showing that 'Twin studies prove no one is born "trapped in the body of the wrong sex"'.

29  Gilligan, A, 'Trans groups under fire for huge rise in child referrals', *The Sunday Times*, 25 November, 2018, https://www.thetimes.co.uk/

So they claim to be transgender. At that point, all too often, efforts to explore and treat the other symptoms may be resisted. But those deeper problems won't go away. They won't be solved by a parent allowing the child to 'change gender'.

## 4. Education or Indoctrination?

In 2017, the National Union of Teachers in the United Kingdom called for toddlers as young as two to be taught about transgender issues.[30] In many countries, schools are the 'gateway' by which gender theory can be promoted, whether under the guise of 'sex education' or 'anti-bullying' guidance.

We saw in Chapter 4 that the aim of sexual revolutionaries has been liberation, including the liberation of children from the 'repressive' norms taught by their parents. Such 'liberators' demand the right to teach other people's children about sex. In Germany and Sweden, parents who object to the sex education given to their children don't even have the right to withdraw children from schools and educate them at home.

'Comprehensive sexuality education' assumes that children and young people have the right to sexual pleasure.[31] Non-judgmental or value-free sex education leaves just one moral standard: the giving of consent. Apart from that, nothing can be forbidden as being immoral. Such 'education' presents sex in relentlessly

---

article/trans-groups-under-fire-for-huge-rise-in-child-referrals-2ttm8c0fr (accessed 5 December, 2018).

30  'Teach toddlers about transgender issues, National Union of Teachers say', *The Daily Telegraph*, 18 April, 2017, https://www.telegraph.co.uk/education/2017/04/17/teach-toddlers-transgender-issues-national-union-teachers-say/ (accessed 13 November, 2018)

31  Kuby, Gabrielle, *The Global Sexual Revolution: Destruction of Freedom in the Name of Freedom*, Lifesite, 2015, pp. 212-229.

individualistic terms. Marriage is rarely mentioned. It's all about individual pleasure and fulfilment.

Responsible sex education would teach children and young people the truth: that delaying sex until adulthood and then deferring intimacy until a relationship is secure greatly increases the chances of achieving a satisfying relationship.[32] But all too often, children are simply told, 'only you know when you are ready for sex'. They are presented with a bleak vision of a world where happiness is reduced down to 'me and what I want'. It leaves them in a frightening world. Boundaries have been smashed down, meaning that everyone can be viewed (or feared) as being a potential sex partner. Such sex education encourages young people to experiment. It is not surprising then that in 2017, in one girl's secondary school in London at least a third of the girls in the Sixth Form aged 16-18 had engaged in same-sex (sexual) relationships.[33]

It's not just secondary schools. Activists want to get into primary schools, even nursery schools. But explicit sex education puts concepts and images in a child's mind that the child is too immature to process or understand. It is a form of sex abuse. Those promoting such ideas have been influenced by the depraved ideas of thinkers such as Sigmund Freud and Wilhelm Reich (see Chapter 4). What does this look like in practice?

In 2015, a video clip from a Swedish children's TV channel went global on YouTube, notching up over a million views within a day of being uploaded. It was designed for three to six-year-olds, to teach them about the body and its functions. Cartoons of male and female

---

32 Grossman, Miriam, 'Take it slow because True Love Waits', October 12, 2012, www.miriamgrossmanmd.com/heads-up-parents/ (accessed 30 May, 2019).

33 Thomson, A, 'Children think it's normal to be 'gender-fluid', *The Times*, 12 April 2017, https://www.thetimes.co.uk/article/children-think-it-s-normal-to-be-gender-fluid-v9xj206rz (accessed 3 December 2018).

private parts dance merrily, accompanied by a sexually explicit song. The project manager for the children's TV programme explained:

The song is part of playful learning, which we believe is the best way to teach kids.[34]

The thought of teaching toddlers to sing about sexual organs is utterly perverse.

Sweden is one of the most socially progressive nations on earth. Yet despite decades of politically correct information and legislation, people there are stubbornly heterosexual. Parents still assume that their children will grow up to marry someone of the opposite sex. People still think it's normal to live in father/mother/children families.

Progressives in the Swedish education system fret that this reveals prejudice against alternative lifestyles. They demand that *norm-critical pedagogy* should be embedded at all levels. The two-sex norm must be eliminated. Teachers at pre-schools are warned that if they plan separate activities for boys and girls, then,

this can contribute to upholding and strengthening the two sex-norm and create a risk for children to experience the method of working as unfair or offensive. Make sure there are gender neutral bathrooms so that children don't need to choose between the boys' and girls' toilet.[35]

Pre-schools must have books about 'rainbow families' and give equal treatment to homo, bi, and hetero homes. Equal time must be

34 MTV News, 'This is what sex-ed for children looks like in Sweden'. 13 January 2015, www.mtv.com/news/2048147/swedish-sex-ed-video-genitals-cartoon/ (accessed 19 February 2015).

35 Edsinger, O, 'Queer Theory on the Rise', Lecture delivered at the European Leadership Forum, 21 May, 2018 http://foclonline.org/talk/queer-theory-rise (accessed 1 December, 2018).

allocated to the various family forms. Three year-olds must not be allowed to think that it's natural to marry someone of the opposite sex! The United Nations Convention on the Rights of the Child says that every child has the right, where possible, to know and be brought up by his or her own natural parents.[36] If we are no longer allowed to present the mother/father/children family as normal, we undermine a secure understanding of the world for all children. Children are now told that their daddy may one day choose to become their mummy. *My New Mommy* is the story of little Violet:

> Life is exciting when you're four years old. You are learning new things every day and things are constantly changing. Violet learns all of these things as she faces the biggest change of her life. Her daddy is about to become a mommy. Life for her will never be the same.[37]

*My New Daddy* tells the story of Charles, whose mummy tells him one day that 'nature made a mistake' and that she should have been born a boy like Charlie:

> Daddy [*aka* mummy] goes to see a doctor and has an operation. Charles now has a new daddy who loves him, and he loves his daddy.[38]

---

36  *The United Nations Convention on the Rights of the Child*, 1989, Article 7, Section 1.

37  Mossiano, L, *My New Mommy*, CreateSpace Independent Publishing Platform, 2012, https://lillymossiano.wordpress.com/books/my-new-mommy/ (accessed 7 December 2018).

38  Mossiano, L, *My New Daddy*, CreateSpace Independent Publishing Platform, 2013, https://lillymossiano.wordpress.com/books/my-new-daddy/ (accessed 7 December 2018).

There could be no surer way of confusing little children! This fairy-tale version of what it's like to have a parent 'transition' bears no relation to the sad reality.[39]

Confusion ensues when little children are told that girls may 'really' be boys. In 2017, a six-year-old boy who lived on the Isle of Wight (off the South Coast of England) was perplexed and upset when another boy in his primary school class was allowed to come in dressed as a girl. His parents were accused of being transphobic when they removed him from school because of the distress this was causing him.[40] A documentary that same year had filmed an 'experiment' on the Isle of Wight where a primary school forced girls and boys to share toilet facilities. Many children registered disgust. Some girls avoided going to the toilet at school altogether – a clear health risk. But the academic who was organising this scheme was confident that, in time, children would just get used to it.[41]

Children are sent to school to be educated, not confused. Yet in some countries, the lie of gender ideology is being imposed on vulnerable and impressionable children. In addition to the sex education within the curriculum, LGBT organisations often offer to go into schools with 'anti-bullying' programmes. These spread the message that children may be 'born in the wrong body'. They may use visual aids such as the 'genderbread person' (see Chapter 3)

---

39   Shick, D, 'When My Father Told Me He Wanted to Be a Woman', *Public Discourse*, 27 March 2015, http://www.thepublicdiscourse.com/2015/03/14661/ (accessed 19 September 2017).

40   'Parents remove son from school in pupil gender row', BBC News 11 September 2017, https://www.bbc.co.uk/news/uk-england-hampshire-41224146 (accessed 5 December 2018).

41   'No more boys and girls, can our children go gender free?' BBC 2, July 2017, https://www.bbc.co.uk/programmes/b09202lp (accessed 3 December 2018).

to teach children they may have a 'gender identity' different from their biological sex, and that it is their 'right' to live according to that identity. 'Gendered Intelligence' is a campaign group which receives public funding in the UK. They visit schools and give presentations to children. They aim to give:

> information about coming out/disclosing, transitioning, your rights as a trans child, teenager, or young adult, how to negotiate life post-transition, and more. [42]

This is, effectively, coaching children into how to demand that their parents and others 'affirm' them in a 'gender identity' which may bear no relation to their biological sex. It is no accident that there has been a dramatic rise in the numbers of children claiming to be 'born in the wrong body'. In the last decade, the Tavistock Clinic in London has seen an increase of 1,173% in referrals of boys, and a 4,415% increase in referrals of girls. [43]

## 5. Don't use Children as Political Pawns

Miranda Yardley is a transsexual who argues that the concept of 'the transgender child' is especially useful to adult campaigners. Transgender activists know that the public is unlikely to be sympathetic to the claims of men whose transgender identity is linked with sexual desire. To shift focus away from those adolescent or adult natal males who experience a tendency to be sexually aroused by the thought of themselves as female (sometimes described as 'autogynephilia'), it is politically expedient to focus

---

42  Youth Work, *Gendered Intelligence*, http://genderedintelligence.co.uk/support/trans-youth/groups (accessed 5 December, 2018).

43  Maynard, Lily, 'The Ethics of Transgender Healtcare', http://lilymaynard.com/first-do-no-harm-the-ethics-of-transgender-healthcare/ (accessed 29 May, 2019). The chart on p. 108 reproduces information from the chart featured on this webpage.

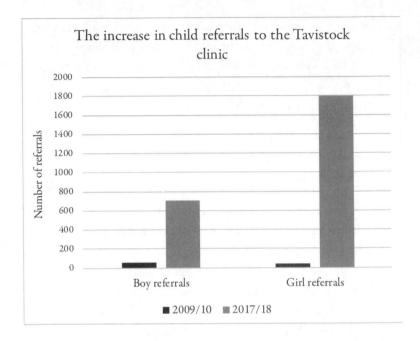

The increase in child referrals to the Tavistock clinic

Number of referrals

■ 2009/10   ■ 2017/18

on the 'needs' of children. Eroticism and sexual desire can be downplayed. Children are being used as a human shield by adult activists.[44]

# 6. What can parents do?

## Teach children and young people God's good design

We need to teach our children that we have not evolved by chance. We are not just 'higher animals'. God created man and woman in His own image: Human beings are exceptionally unique and all human life is to be valued and protected. God created men and women different by design. Knowing we are created by God as

---

44   Yardley, Miranda, 'A Full Life Uninterrupted by Transition', in Brunskell-Evans, H, and Moore, M, Eds., *Transgender Children: Born in your Own Body,* Cambridge Scholars Publishing, 2018, p. 158.

male or female is good news. It liberates us from the pressure of having to construct our own gender identity. We may be different from others in all sorts of ways – we may have our own interests, hobbies, taste in clothes or music etc. But the one reality of being male or female is not a choice.[45] We need to encourage children and young people to respect their bodies, as we are all created by God. We live in an age which puts cruel pressure on young people to focus on how they look. We need to reassure our children that each one is special to God. Our value and dignity does not rest on how other people judge our appearance.

## Teach your child that everyone should be treated kindly, no matter how they behave or what they believe

But teach them also that we should not be forced to agree with the beliefs or actions of others. Disagreement is not hatred. All bullying is wrong, but that means also that our religious or conscientious beliefs should be respected by others.

## Avoid over-exaggerated stereotypes of masculinity and femininity

We live in an age which has tried to get rid of gender stereotypes. Women are told they can do everything men can do. Yet ironically, if children don't fit in with accepted gender stereotypes (for example, girls not wanting to dress in 'pretty' clothes), they may be told that they are not 'really' a girl or a boy. Stephanie Davies-Arai, founder of *Transgender Trend* (a group representing parents and others who are critical of the trend to 'transition' children), writes:

---

45  Richards C, and Jones E, *True Love: what the Bible says about relationships and marriage*, Evangelical Press. See also Lovewise resources: http://lovewise.org.uk/

In increasing numbers, boys who love princess culture become 'girls' and short-haired football-loving girls become 'boys'. Promoted as a 'progressive' social justice movement based on 'accepting difference', transgender ideology in fact takes that difference and stamps it out. It says that the sexist stereotypes of 'gender' are the true distinction between boys and girls and biological sex is an illusion. In this ideology, 'being feminine' has replaced being female as the very definition of 'girl'.[46]

Pink frilly skirts. Blue dinosaur t-shirts. Pink bikes. Blue bikes. This is a fantastic way to increase profits for those marketing clothes, toys, décor, even tableware. In rich Western nations, a family with a boy and a girl may end up buying everything twice! From the cradle up, babies, toddlers, children are pushed into gendered preferences. Those children who don't naturally conform are then 'labelled' as gender-confused.

By contrast, until relatively recently (and still in many countries), families could 'hand down' clothes between girls and boys without too much difficulty; and toys and games were often interchangeable, too.

Superficial cultural expectations can be enforced in an unhelpful way. Just because a little boy is unusually artistic and gentle does not mean that he should be pushed into thinking of himself as homosexual or transsexual. A little girl may be sporty and tomboyish, but that doesn't mean that she should be pushed into identifying herself as lesbian or 'trans'. Behaviours that would have been accepted as within the normal range even a few years ago (girls wanting to play boys' games or boys not wanting to engage in rough-and-tumble games) are now being interpreted as 'gender

46   Davies-Arai, S, 'The Transgender Experiment on Children', Brunskell-Evans, H, and Moore, M, Eds, *Transgender Children: Born in your Own Body*, p. 17.

confusion'. This defies common sense. All children are different, with differing aptitudes and gifts. Parents have the responsibility of encouraging their children's gifts, even when those gifts may not be 'stereotypically' male or female.

## Check out what your child is learning at school

Parents should resist explicit and permissive sex education. Children before puberty should be allowed to be innocent. It is abusive to expose them to sexual activity or images before their brains and bodies are ready.

> For prepubescent boys and girls, sexual things are asleep. The phrase 'sexual awakening' is often used to describe the time in a young person's life when he or she discovers sexual interests. The term 'awakening' implies that something was asleep, and indeed, for younger children this is an accurate observation. Little boys' and girls' bodies look much the same, and they reflect the sexual immaturity of their minds. They may be curious about their own bodies, and the bodies of their parents, or have questions about where babies come from, but they lack the interest and physical development that defines a human being who is equipped for sex and childbearing. Puberty is the time of life when boys and girls begin to physically change and develop into adults with sexual desires.[47]

## Check out what your child is reading and watching

Children aged between about eight and thirteen are often going to be 'best friends' with someone of the same sex. Such friendships may be close, and that is totally normal. Up until the 1950s, children's fiction presented close friendships in a healthy and non-sexualised way.

---

47   McIlhaney, J. A. Jr., and McKissic Bush, F, *Hooked: New Science on how casual sex is affecting our children*, Northfield Publishing, 2008, pp. 13-14.

No longer. In a sexualised culture, children's friendships are being sexualised as well. Much of the fiction promoted by schools now gives children the message that intimate friendship must have romantic or sexual overtones. Children are being told at an ever- younger age they must 'identify' whether they are romantically or emotionally attached to girls or boys or both – i.e., whether they are lesbian, gay or 'bi' (see the genderbread person, Chapter 3). Can't we let children be children?

## Help children and young people to be critical of the claims of gender theory

We need to help young people challenge the assumptions of gender identity theory. We can discuss questions such as 'Do we really have to accept what people think in their minds that they are? How far must this go?'

In 2017, Rachel Dolezal, a white American woman, was found to be wrongly claiming to be black. Logically, if we can choose our gender, why not our race?

In 2018, a sixty-nine-year-old Dutchman went to court to claim the right to 'self-identify' as a forty-nine-year-old. Logically, if we can choose our gender, why not our age?

It may be helpful to discuss with young people the widely circulated short film of interviews with students at Washington University. The demand to accept every claim one might make about one's own identity is exposed as being totally ridiculous. [48]

---

48  'College Kids Say the Darndest Things: On Identity', Family Policy Institute of Washington, see https://www.youtube.com/watch?v=xfO1veFs6Ho as of 18 July 2016.

## Don't be intimidated by threats of suicide

False statistics are routinely repeated.[49] Walt Heyer turns that around by arguing that those who transition are still often likely to commit suicide.[50]

Parents should remember that there's a totally natural and completely safe way of resolving childhood gender confusion. It's called puberty. When children do genuinely experience discontent with their biological sex, if puberty is allowed to take its natural course – and you allow testosterone to kick in for boys, and estrogen for girls – in the vast majority of cases, gender confusion is resolved. Children and young people are impressionable and immature. We don't allow them to make big decisions in other areas. In many countries, they are not allowed to drink alcohol or smoke or get a tattoo until they are 18 or even older. Some experts say that young people's brains are not fully wired up for mature forward thinking until they are 25.

## Your child may thank you for resisting their demands!

Sarah is a nineteen-year-old living in the American Midwest. Between the ages of 14 and 16 she insisted that she should be addressed as a boy. She hated her mum for resisting her demands. She accused her mum of 'dead-naming' her (i.e. using her female name). She was furious that her mum didn't let her bind her breasts or take hormones or apply for breast removal surgery. She constantly posted online about how abusive her mum was. But

---

49 'Transgender Day of Remembrance', Christian Voice, 16 November 2018, https://www.christianvoice.org.uk/index.php/transgender-day-of-remembrance-seriously/ (accessed 1 December 2018).

50 '50 Years of Sex Changes, Mental Disorders, and Too Many Suicides', Public Discourse, February 2016, see http://winst.us7.list-manage2.com/track/click?u=776f667a54759f3894cdd0eee&id=d083940a0c&e=a124a06b84 (accessed 12 May 2017).

now she realises that she never was a boy – she was dissatisfied with the stereotypes, expectations and constraints of being a girl. She says:

> Teen girls are taught to hate everything about themselves. None of us can win! Even the thinnest, most clear skinned, prettiest of girls find an enemy in the mirror.[51]

She's so glad now that her mum resisted her demands.

In 2018, a group of professionals and others contributed to a symposium entitled *Transgender Children: Born in Your Own Body*. They all challenge the trend towards affirming the desire of some children to 'change sex', and agree that:

> Transgendering children is not progressive, but politically reactionary, medically dangerous, and abusive of children.[52]

## Further Reading

Heather Brunskell-Evans, and Michele Moore, eds., *Transgender Children: Born in Your Own Body*, Cambridge Scholars Publishing, 2018. (This is a symposium by a variety of contributors, not from a Christian perspective, but questioning the current trend towards affirming the desire of some children to 'change sex'.)

---

51  Sarah R, 'I hated her guts at the time: A trans-desister and her mom tell their story', *4thwavenow*, 18 January, 2018, https://4thwavenow.com/2018/01/18/i-hated-her-guts-at-the-time-a-trans-desister-and-her-mom-tell-their-story/amp/?__twitter_impression=true (accessed 16 November 2018).

52  Brunskell-Evans, H, and Moore, M, Eds., *Transgender Children: Born in your Own Body*, p. 3. An online summary is available here: http://www.cambridgescholars.com/download/sample/64273 as of 16 November 2018.

# 7.
# How Should we Respond?
# A Call to Respect

**P**eople such as Walt Heyer are passionately concerned with protecting others from the dangerous idea that we can change gender. At the beginning of this book, we saw from his testimony that:

- *Gender confusion involves deep unhappiness, and those who suffer from it are not necessarily trying to promote an ideology*
- *We should treat everyone with kindness and respect*
- *Real kindness means believing and telling the truth*
- *We need to understand the ideas behind the claim that we can 'change sex'*

Having examined the claims of gender theory, we can see that it demonstrates profound disrespect for the human body, which means contempt for human dignity. Demanding medical interventions to alter healthy bodies also reveals a disrespect for the natural 'ecology' of humanity. Such demands for medical intervention (while at the same time denying that gender incongruence is an illness!) leads to disrespect for the conscience of medical professionals who don't want to damage healthy bodies.

The idea that you can believe what small children claim about themselves – and allow them, on that basis, to launch down a track that almost invariably leads to life-changing and damaging interventions, reveals deep disrespect for the vulnerability of children. Equally, when outside 'experts', whether teachers or social workers, go over the heads of parents to encourage children and young children to 'explore their gender identity', this manifests profound disrespect for the rights of parents.

To say that by claiming to be men or women, people who are not biologically male or female can enter (for example) men's or women's changing rooms involves disrespect for privacy and safety.

All too often, those who want to question gender theory are shouted down as 'bigots' and 'transphobes', which shows disrespect for freedom of speech. Those who regret their transition often have to remain anonymous because of hostility from activists who display disrespect for their testimony.

Denying that humankind is fundamentally binary disrespects the entire history of humanity and defies truth. And rejecting belief in the creation design for male and female disrespects God Himself. By contrast, we conclude this book with a ten-fold call to respect.

## 1. Respect human dignity

The trans-affirming movement insists that human dignity is only respected when we accept the premise that we are autonomous (on the basis that there is no Creator God, so we can determine who we are and how we live). In reality, human dignity is only respected when we understand that we are made by God, in His image. We must be careful, even in casual conversation, not to joke about, mock, or belittle people who are trans or suffering any degree of gender confusion. We are to treat everyone with civility and respect.

There is huge pressure from the culture, and even from within the evangelical church, to accept and affirm individuals' own claims about their identity, especially if they are clearly suffering deep anguish. But, as in every pastoral interaction, true compassion has to be grounded in God's good design for humanity. Our Creator has revealed His will for human flourishing. Testimonies from those who transition and who, sometimes many years later, regret it, point to the false compassion of affirming transition. They agree that when someone in the church affirmed their transition (including using the name and pronouns they demand), it provided the euphoria of acceptance. Yet, deep down, peace with God was not going to be found until truth was confronted.

Affirming people in their false perception of their own identity leads to further confusion about sex and gender. Our identity is not to be understood in terms of 'feeling', but rather in terms of 'calling'. God has called us to live either as men or women, and His calling meshes with the way that He has created us. We don't underestimate the challenge that it will be for some to live out that calling. Some Christians offer a superficial and false hope that all gender confusion will be resolved in this life. But in a fallen world, where creation itself is still 'groaning', we all suffer from a variety of conditions and temptations. Complete liberation from these is promised at the resurrection, when we are given glorified bodies. But in this life in the long-term, to 'choose' an identity contrary to our created reality will only cause deeper distress.

There are various reasons why an individual may feel a measure of unease with their biological sex. Some of those reasons (childhood trauma, for example) may involve having been sinned against, rather than deliberately sinning. But assuming the identity of someone of the opposite sex does involve sin. Real respect for the human body as created by God means that medical interventions – whether hormone treatments or surgery in order to 'reassign gender' – are to be rejected.

Trevor Phillips was chairman of the Equalities and Human Rights Commission in the UK from 2006 to 2012. He argues that extreme trans activists and their allies are adding a new layer of anguish to the suffering of those who are experiencing gender confusion, by 'raising false hopes that changing gender could become as easy as changing a name'.[1] He is right. To go along with the false claims of gender theory is not, ultimately, either loving towards people or respectful of human dignity.

## 2. Respect the 'ecology' of humanity

There is a profound contradiction between the current concern for natural ecology in all other areas, and gender ideology which challenges the binary found in nature. Environmentalists seek to respect nature and resist chemical interventions. But gender theory undermines the 'eco-system' of humanity. Pope Benedict XVI often spoke about 'human ecology':

> Man too has a nature that he must respect and that he cannot manipulate at will. Man is not merely self-creating freedom. Man does not create himself. He is intellect and will, but he is also nature, and his will is rightly ordered if respects nature, listens to it, and accepts himself for who he is, as one who did not create himself.[2]

---

1   Phillips, T, 'Trans activists are putting equality at risk', *The Times*, 22 October, 2018, https://www.thetimes.co.uk/article/trans-extremists-are-putting-equality-at-risk-fjv8skwz0 (accessed 5 December 2018).

2   Quoted in Mattson, D, *Why I Don't Call Myself Gay,* Ignatius Press, 2017, p. 94.

The created order should be respected, not defied.

## 3. Respect the vocation of doctors to 'do no harm'

'First, do no harm', *primum non nocere*, is a basic principle of medical ethics. The job of doctors is to seek health and healing. If doctors conscientiously believe that prescribing puberty blockers, prescribing cross-sex hormones, or performing 'reassignment surgery' will only damage perfectly healthy bodies, their convictions should be respected.

The history of medicine is littered with short-term fads: enthusiasm for interventions that have, with hindsight, been viewed as harmful and ridiculous. For centuries, patients had to endure aggressive 'bleeding', using leeches or other methods. During the nineteenth century, 'blue pills' (*aka* mercury) were prescribed for all manner of illnesses – they made matters worse. In the twentieth century, minor mental illness was 'treated' with radical brain surgery (lobotomy) that was often catastrophically damaging. For a while, there was a fashion for removing perfectly healthy teeth (all of them!) as a way of preventing future infections.[3] And so it goes, on and on. We look back with pity for those patients whose suffering was only compounded by doctors. But we'll look back with horror at what is going on now. Jane Galloway, a parent and women's rights campaigner in the UK, warns:

> I fear greatly that in 10 to 15 years' time, we will find ourselves with a slew of young adults with mutilated bodies, no sexual function, who will turn around to the National Health Service and ask: 'Why did you let us do this?'[4]

---

3    Heyer, W, *Paper Genders*, pp. 47-71.

4    Gilligan, A, 'Trans groups under fire for huge rise in child referrals', *The Sunday Times*, 25 November, 2018, https://www.thetimes.co.uk/

We should also not be naive about the extent to which medical professionals are sometimes placed under financial pressure to prescribe elective treatments. There are huge profits to be made for the pharmaceutical industry from the increasing demand for hormone-altering drugs.[5]

## 4. Respect the vulnerability of children

Many of the pioneers of the sexual revolution and gender theory also promoted paedophilia (see Chapter 4). They abused and exploited the natural innocence and vulnerability of the young. We should allow children to grow up secure in their identity as male or female, and we should allow children to be free from sexual exploitation of any kind. That includes freedom from being exploited as political pawns by activists.[6]

Children should also grow up with the security of the ongoing care of their own father and mother; they should not have to face daily uncertainty about whether their 'mum might become their dad' or *vice versa* (see Chapter 6).

Unprecedented numbers of children are being identified as 'transgender', and this is leading to interventions that are damaging medically, emotionally and socially. Walt Heyer writes from bitter experience:

Changing genders is short-term gain with long-term pain. Its consequences include early mortality, regret, mental illness, and

article/trans-groups-under-fire-for-huge-rise-in-child-referrals-2ttm8c0fr (accessed 5 December, 2018).

5    Gomes, Jules, 'Drugs Giants Scent Gold in those transgender teens', *Rebel Priest*, 30 April, 2018, https://www.julesgomes.com/single-post/Drug-giants-scent-gold-in-those-transgender-teens (accessed 24 May, 2019).

6    Brunskell-Evans, H and Moore, M, Eds., *Transgender Children: Born in Your Own Body*, Cambridge Scholars Publishing, 2018, p. 12.

suicide. Instead of encouraging them to undergo unnecessary and destructive surgery, let's affirm and love our young people just the way they are.[7]

Heather Brunskell-Evans, Senior Research Fellow at King's College, London, argues that:

> transgender theory is mythological and ... pernicious not only to the individual children who become identified as transgender but to all children in the school communities to which Gendered Intelligence programmes are delivered.[8]

She predicts that future generations will look back on the current transgender trend with shame.

## 5. Respect the rights of parents

Those promoting gender theory consistently present parents as an 'unsafe' influence on their children if they question this theory. Parents who don't want to affirm the claims of their child to be 'transgender' are portrayed as being transphobic and bigoted.

In February 2018, a judge in Ohio removed a gender dysphoric teenager from the custody of her parents who refused to support 'transition' using hormone therapy.[9] This is terrifying. Parents are far more likely to have the best interests of their child at heart than are representatives of the State. They are also far more likely

---

7   'I was a Transgender Woman', *Public Discourse*, 1 April 2015, http://www. thepublicdiscourse.com/2015/04/14688/ (accessed 12 May 2017).

8   Brunskell-Evans, H, and Moore, M, Eds., *Transgender Children: Born in your Own Body*, pp. 6-7.

9   Walker, A. T, 'Parental Rights: A Casualty of the Transgender Revolution', *Public Discourse*, 26 February, 2018, https://www.thepublicdiscourse. com/2018/02/21122/ (accessed 6 December 2018).

to be the best judges of their own child's capacity to make major decisions.

## 6. Respect the privacy and safety of women and girls

The increasing move to allow 'self-declaration' is posing a great challenge to the ability of females to compete in sports, where the biological differences between men and women mean that sex segregation is necessary in order to create a level playing field. Females are placed at a significant disadvantage in many sports if forced to compete against biological males who identify as female.[10] But allowing men who identify as female to participate in female sports also raises issues of privacy and safety.

We must not be naïve. The tragic reality is that there are sexual predators who have used the legal rights afforded to transsexuals in order to pose as a transsexual person to gain access to female-only facilities in order to abuse girls and women. Ryan Anderson and Melody Wood documented over 130 examples of men charged with using access to female-only spaces in order to carry out voyeurism and sexual assault.[11] We should be especially vigilant about protecting young children in everyday life. For example, parents will want to ensure that young children do not use public toilets unaccompanied if there is a threat to children's safety.

It is reasonable not to want to be seen in a state of undress by a member of the opposite sex (no matter what that person of the

---

10   'A high school girl's life after transgender athletes joined her sport', Daily Signal, 5 May, 2019, https://www.youtube.com/watch?v=NIlq85dL0C4 (accessed 7 June, 2019); 'Sex-segregated Sports and the new IOC Guidlines', *The Feministahood*, 27, January, 2016, https://thefeministahood.wordpress.com/2016/01/27/sex-segregated-sports/#more-399 (accessed 6 June, 2019).

11   Anderson, R, and Wood, M, 'Gender Identity Policies in Schools, What Congress, the Courts and the Trump Administration should do'.

opposite sex says about their 'identity'). It is reasonable not to want to see a member of the opposite sex in a state of undress (no matter what they believe about themselves). Our right to privacy is important, as well as the right to safety. The right to bodily privacy is especially important for any who have been the victims of sexual abuse. But those who point this out are routinely shouted down as 'transphobic' – which leads us to the importance of free speech.

## 7. Respect Free Speech

Natalie Bird had to flee from an abusive partner. She believes that women's refuges should be exactly that – refuges where abused women feel safe from potential attack. When she said that people who are biologically male should not be allowed access to such refuges, she was accused of transphobia – and was forced out of her role in her political party. She responded:

> Standing up for the rights of vulnerable women is nothing I should be ashamed of. The lack of freedom of speech and freedom of thought on this issue is frankly terrifying.[12]

At present, the perceived need to have one's identity as a victim continually affirmed is trumping the right to critical discussion. Feminist campaigner Julie Bindel went to Bristol in April 2018 to speak on proposals for gender recognition. But a group of masked demonstrators blocked her entry to the meeting, and police failed to intervene.[13] Trans intolerance is seemingly unstoppable. But freedom of thought, conscience, speech and religion are

12   Bannerman, L, 'Lib Dem trans activists hounded abuse victim', *The Times*, 19 October, 2018, https://www.thetimes.co.uk/article/lib-dem-trans-activists-hounded-abuse-victim-b6dx39tv3 (accessed 5 December 2018).

13   Myers, F, 'Trans intolerance is out of control', *Spiked Online*, 25 April 2018, https://www.spiked-online.com/2018/04/25/trans-intolerance-is-out-of-control/ (accessed 6 December 2018).

fundamental to a free society. Even those who disagree on other issues should be able to unite to insist on freedom of debate.

## 8. Respect the testimony of those who regret their transition

In November 2018, *The Daily Telegraph* published a tragic letter from someone warning of the current 'trendy to be trans' culture which is pushing many young people into making life-changing decisions. As a young man, the writer of the letter had had 'high hopes of finally realising my teenage dream' when he had had gender reassignment surgery. But the dream unravelled over the years,

> most of all because I cannot entirely escape my male origins. I must accept the harsh reality that no amount of drastic cutting of my body can ever alter my biology.[14]

We should respect those who regret their decision to transition. Sadly, such testimonies of are often either ignored or vilified. Some 'regretters' feel the need to remain anonymous for this reason. But some speak out, including those who can testify that turning back to their Creator God has helped them towards a life of greater integrity and wholeness.[15]

---

14 *The Daily Telegraph*, Letters, 'Trans legislation will endanger the Young', 29 November 2019, https://www.telegraph.co.uk/opinion/2018/11/29/letters-theresa-mays-attempt-push-brexit-deal-parliament-affront/ (accessed 6 December 2018).

15 Shick, D, *Understanding Gender Confusion: A Faith-based Perspective*, Help4Families Press, 2014; *Tranzformed: Finding Peace with your God-Given Gender*, 2017, DVD, *PurePassion Media*; Heyer, W, *Trans Life Survivors*, Lightening Source, 2018.

## 9. Respect Truth

Nature exists. Our bodies are created as either male or female. Sex is a reality. Gender is a social manifestation of our sex. The 'subversion of identity' is the subversion of truth. Language is being mangled and distorted. When nurses are told to avoid the term 'breast feeding' and use the term 'chest feeding' instead, truth is being undermined. Female breasts have the capacity to nurse infants; male chests do not. When primary children are told that girls can have a penis, truth is undermined.

## 10. Respect our Creator God

The Bible pictures two ways to live. The way of folly is to ignore our Creator God and defy His laws. The way of wisdom is to fear (respect and honour) the Lord. Rightful respect for God the Creator means giving Him thanks for His good creation, and bearing witness to others of the goodness of His creation. It is God Himself who forms us in our mother's womb; we are not accidents of evolution (Ps. 139:13). The lie of gender theory has already harmed many people, including children and young people. Many are scared to speak out for fear of being labelled 'transphobic'. Many are intimidated into speaking what they know to be untrue – in the interests of not causing offence. But we are to obey God rather than men (Acts 5:29). We may be tempted to follow the example of those who turned back from following Christ because 'they loved the glory that comes from man more than the glory that comes from God' (John 12:43). But we should remember that:

> The fear of man lays a snare, but whoever trusts in the LORD is safe (Prov. 29:25).

Respect for God means holding to the truth, and it also means extending His free offer of grace to those who have been deceived by lies. To all those who struggle, including those who weary of having to 'perform' a role that is alien to their biological identity, Jesus Christ extends both an invitation and a promise:

> Come to me, all who labour and are heavy laden, and I will give you rest. Take my yoke upon you, and learn from me, for I am gentle and lowly in heart, and you will find rest for your souls. For my yoke is easy, and my burden is light (Matt. 11:28-30).

> A bruised reed he will not break, and a smouldering wick he will not quench (Matt. 12:20).

Our Creator God both shows us the way to live wisely, and freely offers grace to all those who struggle.

## Conclusion

Gender theory is a lie. To be sure, some ideas around masculinity and femininity are socially constructed, but that does not mean that maleness or femaleness is arbitrarily assigned at birth, or that it is something that can be affirmed independent of one's biological sex. Our culture is increasingly embracing gender theory, and it is shaping its legal and educational system in its light. But we need to hold on to the truth and to do so in a way that is informed and compassionate and which communicates the goodness of God's truth for everyone.

## Further Reading

Anderson, R, *When Harry Became Sally: Responding to the Transgender Moment*, Encounter Books, 2018.

# Further Resources

## Organisations

*Help 4 Families* http://help4families.com/ (Christian support groups for parents based in the U.S.)

*Lovewise*, https://lovewise.org.uk/ (Biblical resources for children, young people, and parents)

*Sex Change Regret* www.sexchangeregret.com/ (A website for support of those who have transitioned and who later regret it.)

*Transgender Trend*, https://www.transgendertrend.com/ (A group of 'parents questioning the trans narrative'; not a Christian group)

## Briefings/Books/Papers

Anderson, R, *When Harry Became Sally: Responding to the Transgender Moment*, Encounter Books, 2018

Brunskell-Evans, H and Moore, M, eds., *Transgender Children: Born in your Own Body*, Cambridge Scholars Publishing, 2018

(This is a symposium by a variety of contributors. Although not written from a Christian perspective, it questions the current trend towards affirming the desire of some children to 'change sex'. An online summary is available here: http://www.cambridgescholars.com/download/sample/64273 [time-limited])

Congregation for Catholic Education, *Male and Female He Created Them, Towards a Path of Dialogue on the question of Gender Theory in Education*, Vatican City, 2019, (Catholic Truth Society), also available online: https://www.lifesitenews.com/images/local/CONGREGATION_ FOR_CATHOLIC_EDUCATION_EN.pdf

The Christian Institute, *Transsexualism* www.christian.org.uk/ resource/transsexualism-briefing

The Christian Institute, *Radical Gender Ideology: Protect your Child*, available on request.

The Christian Institute, *Gnosticism* http://www.christian.org.uk/ wp-content/uploads/gnosticism.pdf

Cretella, M, Van Meter, Q, McHugh, P, 'Gender Ideology Harms Children', March 2016, American College of Pediatricians, April 6, 2016, http://www.acpeds.org/the-college-speaks/position-statements/ gender-ideology-harms-children

Cretella, M, 'I'm a Pediatrician. How Transgender Ideology has Infiltrated my Field and Produced Large-Scale Child Abuse', *The Daily Signal*, 3 July, 2017, https://www.dailysignal.com/2017/07/03/im-pediatrician-transgender-ideology-infiltrated-field-produced-large-scale-child-abuse/

Fogarty, Taylor, 'What two former trans men want you to know about all the lies', *The Federalist*, 11 October 2017, https://www.thefederalist.com/2017/10/11/what-two-former-trans-men-want-you-to-know-about-all-the-lies

Francis B, and Ballantyne J, 'Where Angels Fear to Tread: The Fraud of Transgenderism', *Public Discourse*, 14 November, 2018, https://www.thepublicdiscourse.com/2018/11/42698/

Heyer, W, *Paper Genders: Pulling the Mask Off the Transgender Phenomenon*, Make Waves, 2011

Heyer, W, *Kid Dakota and the Secret at Grandma's House*, CreateSpace Independent Publishing, 2015

Heyer, W, *Trans Life Survivors*, 2018

Heyer, W, 'Here's what parents of transgender kids need to know', *The Federalist*, 9 January 2015, http://thefederalist.com/2015/01/09/heres-what-parents-of-transgender-kids-need-to-know/

Heyer, W, '"Sex-Change Surgery": What Bruce Jenner, Dianne Sawyer and You Should Know', *Public Discourse*, 27 April 2015, http://www.thepublicdiscourse.com/2015/04/14905/

Heyer, W, 'I was a Transgender Woman', *Public Discourse*, 1 April 2015, http://www.thepublicdiscourse.com/2015/04/14688/

Heyer, W, 'Fifty Years of Sex Changes, Mental Disorders, and Too Many Suicides', *Public Discourse*, February 2016, https://www.thepublicdiscourse.com/2016/02/16376/

James, S, 'What is the Transgender Agenda and how should Christians respond?' *Reformation Today*, 280, November/December 2017 http://www.reformation-today.org/articles-of-interest/what-is-the-transgender-agenda-and-how-should-christians-respond/

James, S, *God's Design for Women in an Age of Gender Confusion*, Evangelical Press, 2019

Kuby, G, *The Global Sexual Revolution: Destruction of Freedom in the Name of Freedom*, LifeSite, 2015

Lopez, R O and Klein, B, *Jephthah's Children: The Innocent Casualties of Same-Sex Parenting*, Wilberforce Publications, 2016

Mayer, Lawrence S, McHugh, Paul R, Sexuality and Gender: Findings from the Biological, Psychological and Social Sciences, *The New Atlantis, Special Report*, Fall 2016, https://www.thenewatlantis.com/publications/introduction-sexuality-and-gender

Martin, D, *Rewriting Gender? You, Your Family, Transgenderism and the Gospel*, Christian Focus, 2018

McHugh, P, 'Transgender Surgery Isn't the Solution', *Wall Street Journal*, 12 June 2014

McHugh, P, 'Surgical Sex: Why We Stopped Doing Sex Change Operations', *First Things*, November 2004, http://www.firstthings.com/article/2004/11/surgical-sex

Nolland, L, ed., *The New Normal: The Transgender Agenda*, Wilberforce Publications, 2018

Mohler, A, *We Cannot Be Silent*, Nelson, 2015

Pearcey, N, *Love Thy Body: Answering Hard Questions about Life and Sexuality*, Baker, 2018

'Sarah R', 'I Hated Her Guts At The Time: A Trans-desister and Her Mom Tell Their Story', *4thwavenow*, 18 January, 2018, https://4thwavenow.com/2018/01/18/i-hated-her-guts-at-the-time-a-trans-desister-and-her-mom-tell-their-story/amp/?__twitter_impression=true

Seagraves, B and Leavine, H, *Gender – A Conversation Guide for Parents and Pastors*, The Good Book Company, 2017.

Shick, D, *Understanding Gender Confusion: A Faith Based Perspective*, CreateSpace, 2014

Shick, D, *Transgender Confusion: A Biblical Based Q & A For Families*, CreateSpace, 2016

Stanton, G, *Boys, Girls, Other: Making Sense of the Confusing New World of Gender Identity*, Family First New Zealand, 2015, https://askmefirst.nz/wp-content/uploads/2016/08/Boys-Girls-Other-FULL-REPORT.pdf

Tinker, Melvin, *That Hideous Strength: How the West was Lost: The Cancer of Cultural Marxism in the Church, the World and the Gospel of Change*, Evangelical Press, 2018

Van Gend, D, *Stealing from A Child: The Injustice of 'Marriage Equality'*, Connor Court Publishing, 2016

Walker, A, *God and the Transgender Debate*, The Good Book Company, 2017

## Video clips/DVDs

Washington students interviewed about identity: http://christiannews.net/2016/04/16/video-college-students-polled-on-identity-agree-short-white-man-can-identify-as-tall-chinese-woman/

*Tranzformed: Finding Peace with Your God-Given Gender*, 2017, DVD, PurePassion Media

# Christian Focus Publications

Our mission statement —

STAYING FAITHFUL

In dependence upon God we seek to impact the world through literature faithful to His infallible Word, the Bible. Our aim is to ensure that the Lord Jesus Christ is presented as the only hope to obtain forgiveness of sin, live a useful life and look forward to heaven with Him.

Our books are published in four imprints:

### CHRISTIAN
## FOCUS

Popular works including basic doctrine, biographies, commentaries, and Christian living.

### CHRISTIAN
## HERITAGE

Books representing some of the best material from the rich heritage of the church.

## MENTOR

Books written at a level suitable for Bible College and seminary students, pastors, and other serious readers. The imprint includes commentaries, doctrinal studies, examination of current issues and church history.

## CF4•K

Children's books for quality Bible teaching and for all age groups: Sunday school curriculum, puzzle and activity books; personal and family devotional titles, biographies and inspirational stories — because you are never too young to know Jesus!

Christian Focus Publications Ltd,
Geanies House, Fearn, Ross-shire,
IV20 1TW, Scotland, United Kingdom.
www.christianfocus.com